Languedoc: Carcassonne to Montpellier

Dana Facaros & Michael Pauls

Credits

Footprint credits

Editor: Alan Murphy
Production and layout: Angus Dawson
Maps: Kevin Feeney

Managing Director: Andy Riddle
Content Director: Patrick Dawson
Publisher: Alan Murphy
Publishing Managers: Felicity Laughton, Jo Williams, Nicola Gibbs
Marketing and Partnerships Director: Liz Harper
Marketing Executive: Liz Eyles
Trade Product Manager: Diane McEntee
Account Managers: Paul Bew, Tania Ross
Advertising: Renu Sibal, Elizabeth Taylor
Finance: Phil Walsh

Photography credits
Front cover: Richard Semik/Dreamstime
Back cover: Marketa Buskova

Printed in Great Britain by CPI Antony Rowe, Chippenham, Wiltshire

Publishing information
Footprint *Focus Languedoc: Carcassonne to Montpellier*
1st edition
© Footprint Handbooks Ltd
April 2012

ISBN: 978 1 908206 58 9
CIP DATA: A catalogue record for this book is available from the British Library

® Footprint Handbooks and the Footprint mark are a registered trademark of Footprint Handbooks Ltd

Published by Footprint
6 Riverside Court
Lower Bristol Road
Bath BA2 3DZ, UK
T +44 (0)1225 469141
F +44 (0)1225 469461
footprinttravelguides.com

Distributed in the USA by Globe Pequot Press, Guilford, Connecticut

The content of Footprint *Focus Languedoc: Carcassonne to Montpellier* has been extracted from Footprint's *Languedoc* guide, which was researched and written by Dana Facaros & Michael Pauls.

Contents

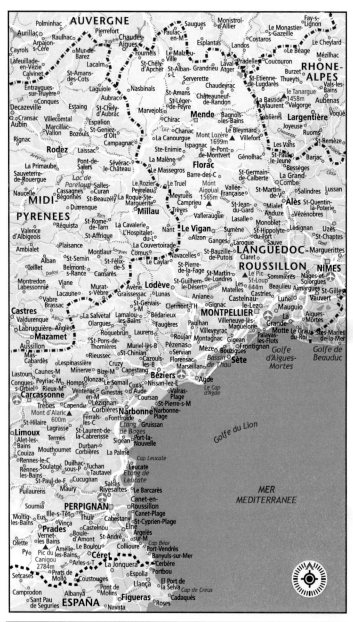

Carcassonne to Montpellier encompasses the départements of the Aude and Hérault, the very heart of Languedoc, with all the essential Languedoc ingredients: the vertiginous Cathar castles tickling the clouds, the Canal du Midi winding lazily through sun soaked hills covered with vines. Sandy beaches that stretch for miles on end, some wild, others like Cap d'Agde full of fashionable Parisians. Inland, medieval villages huddle around Romanesque abbeys, high over gorges where rivers made kayaking, rush down to the Mediterranean from the Massif Centrale.

As Provence fills up with glitterati, Languedoc basks in its reputation as 'the thinking person's south of France.' In recent years, fairy tale Carcassonne, with its World Heritage crown of walls and towers has been a chief beneficiary of the growth of low cost European flights; as a key gateway to Languedoc, it now has a panoply of boutique hotels and gastronomic restaurants. While Carcassonne perfects its charms, Montpellier, charges full steam ahead: the capital of the Languedoc region as well as a major university, medical and research centre, hosting a full calendar of top-notch music, theatre, dance, cinema and art events, it's the fastest growing and most future-oriented city in France. Yet in the midst of all this go-getting is a lovely 17th-18th century core, filled with elegant *hôtels particuliers*, boutiques and bars, as well as one of the finest art museums outside of Paris.

In between these two cities, Languedoc offers plenty to see and do as you'll discover in this little book. But also take time to enjoy what many people love best about the region: the laid-back pace of life (outside of Montpellier, that is!), the old fashioned friendliness in the village cafés, exploring the local vineyards and weekly markets overflowing with fresh local produce…and the joy of just lazing about in the Languedoc sun.

Planning your trip

Places to visit in Languedoc: Carcassonne to Montpellier

The Aude

The Aude, as its slogan proclaims, is 'the land of the Cathars' and interest in the area, piqued by bestsellers, has made it quite popular in recent years. Its capital Carcassonne, a glorious fairytale vision, can get so busy that you'll need to carefully time your visit to avoid the crowds. On the other hand, you'll need your walking shoes for the other Cathar castles – the ruined, outrageously picturesque last refuges of Languedoc's medieval heretics. Most of these are in the rugged Corbières south of Carcassonne, an area synonymous with red wine. Lovers of bubbly, however, shouldn't miss Limoux. The curious flock to the vortex of French mysteries, Rennes-le-Château; the adventurous go whitewater rafting down the Aude; and the palaeontology buffs visit Dinosauria in Espéraza. The Canal du Midi passes through the area (although for convenience's sake we've included it all in the Hérault chapter), and one of its branches, the Canal de la Robine, transverses Narbonne. This was the Roman capital of Languedoc and once the seat of a powerful bishop, with a stunning cathedral complex to prove it and a museum worthy of the Cardinal's palaces in Rome. One of the greatest religious houses of Languedoc, the Abbaye de Fontfroide, is nearby, whilst just over the coastal mountain of La Clape await a string of beaches and the excellent safari park at Sigean.

The Hérault

At the heart of Languedoc, the Hérault is home to the region's feverish capital and its biggest university. Montpellier's beautifully restored historic centre, L'Ecusson, bursts at the seams with sophisticated *hôtels particuliers*, boutiques, trendy hotels and restaurants, and the region's top art collection, the Musée Fabre. Nearby Pézenas, the elegant former capital, takes pride in its association with Molière. There's a long swathe of coast, with the vibrant port of Sète and great shellfish nursery of the Bassin de Thau in the middle, and two hugely popular beach resorts on either end – the bodacious, Jetsons-friendly La Grande Motte and the fashionable Le Cap d'Agde, built near an ancient Greek colony and with museums containing stunning ancient bronzes found in nearby shipwrecks. The Hérault's amiable second city, Béziers, is piled under its enormous cathedral, near the hilltop Oppidum d'Ensérune, the most impressive of the pre-Greek and Roman cities of Languedoc. The most fascinating stretch of the Canal du Midi begins near here as well, before passing through a series of delightful canal ports. The hilly limestone *garrigue* that dominates the northern Hérault is endowed with wild gorges, Minervois vineyards and beautiful villages, such as St-Guilhem-le-Désert, Minerve, Roquebrun and Orlagues.

Getting to Languedoc: Carcassonne to Montpellier

Air

Flights from the UK and Ireland go to the regional airports of Montpellier, Bézier-Cap d'Agde, and Carcassonne. These are especially well served in summer by Ryanair, departing from Birmingham, Bournemouth, Bristol, Cork, Dublin, East Midlands, Manchester, Glasgow Prestwick, Leeds Bradford, Liverpool, Luton, and London Stansted,. There are also direct flights with EasyJet to Montpellier from Gatwick and Flybe to Béziers from Southampton. Other flights (also on British Airways, Easyjet, Air France and Jet2) serve airports close to Languedoc, notably Toulouse and Avignon.

From North America There are no direct flights to Languedoc-Roussillon from America. **Air Canada**, **Air France**, **British Airways**, **Delta** and **United Airlines** fly into Paris Charles de Gaulle International Airport, where you can pick up direct Air France flights to Montpellier or Toulouse. Often the best deal from North America is to fly into Montpellier or Toulouse via Amsterdam, Munich or Frankfurt on **KLM** or **Lufthansa**.

From the rest of Europe There are direct flights from Paris (Charles de Gaulle and Orly), Lyon and Nantes in France, and from Frankfort, Munich Brussels (Charloi) Madrid and Copenhagen to Montpellier. Carcassonne airport also has connections with Brussels (Charloi), Porto, and Billund-Denmark; Béziers has links from Paris Beauvais, Oslo Rygge, Stockholm, and Düsseldorf Weeze. Other options to look at are the flights from most of Europe to both Toulouse and Marseille – or hop on a train (see below).

Airport information Aéroport Montpellier Méditerranée ① *T04 67 20 85 00, montpellier. aeroport.fr*, is 8 km from the centre of Montpellier. A regular shuttle bus (No. 120) runs from the airport to the Place de l'Europe, where there's a station serving the city's two tramway lines. Contact Hérault Transport (T04 34 88 89 99).
    Aéroport Béziers Cap d'Agde ① *T04 67 80 99 09, beziers.aeroport.fr*, is located between Béziers and Agde. A shuttle (No. 210) coincides with flights, going to Béziers' bus and train stations (€3.10) and to Marseillan (€4); see schedule on the airport website.
    Aéroport Carcassonne ① *T04 68 71 96 46, aeroport-carcassonne.com*, is linked by the Navette Agglo'bus Aeroport (T04 68 47 82 22, tickets €5, available on board) to Carcassonne, the train station, the Ville Basse and the medieval Cité. The shuttles run to coincide with each flight.
    Aéroport Toulouse-Blagnac ① *T08 25 38 00 00, toulouse.aeroport.fr*, has shuttle connections (navette-tisseo-aeroport.com, €5) every 20-40 minutes with the centre of Toulouse and the train station.

Rail
Travelling by **Eurostar** ① *T08 432 186 186, eurostar.com*, and **TGV** ① *tgv-europe.com*, from London to Montpellier takes just over 7 hours. After an easy change in Paris – from Gare du Nord to the Gare de Lyon, take the RER D – it's non-stop. Contact Eurostar and use the TGV website to arrange the journey independently, or contact **European Rail** ① *T020-7619 1083, europeanrail.com*, and let them do it all. Note that with the TGV's Prem's fares you can get big discounts by booking up to 90 days before you travel.

Road
Car London to Montpellier is just over 1000 km and the drive can be done in a day if you start early. Once you get to Paris, there are three main autoroutes south. The most direct is the A10 to Orléans, the A71 to Vierzon and the A75 down to Languedoc (6½ hrs, tolls €40), which includes crossing the magnificent Viaduc de Millau.
    For Carcassonne, , it's faster to pick up the A20 in Vierzon to Toulouse and then the A61 (7 hrs to Carcassonne, tolls €40).
    To bring a GB-registered car into France you need your vehicle registration document, full driving licence and insurance certificate, which must be carried at all times when

driving, along with your passport. You'll need to adjust or tape the headlamps, and carry a warning triangle and safety vest inside the car (not the boot).

The lowest rate for seven days' **car hire** starts at around €200. If you're travelling with kids and a lot of bags, it's probably cheaper to drive and easier to bring your own car. Otherwise, what works best for you depends on the time of year, what fly/drive or rail/drive deals you can find, and whether or not you like long drives.

Transport in Languedoc: Carcassonne to Montpellier

If you just want to stick to the main cities, famous sites and beaches, Languedoc-Roussillon's trains and buses are just about good enough to get around. Otherwise, unless you're hiring a canal barge with bicycles or are coming specifically for a walking or riding tour you may well need a car. Every news-stand sells maps of the region – the Michelin or Blay 1:250000 are both good and frequently updated. Trekkers should pick up IGN Série Bleue 1:25000 maps, which can also be bought before arrival (loisirs.ign.fr).

Rail

France's national railway, the **SNCF**, has a very useful online service in English (www.tgv-europe.com) for finding schedules and booking tickets. They also have a toll number, T3635 (€0.34 per min), which can be used throughout France. The website doubles as a tour operator, offering discounts on hotels, ski packages, flights and rental cars, and they'll post tickets outside France. There are a variety of InterRail passes available for all ages (including a France Rail pass that's valid just for France), but they're really only good value if you mean to do several days of long-distance travelling outside the Languedoc-Roussillon region. For more information, visit raileurope.co.uk, if you live outside Europe the website is raileurope.com.

France's sleek trains, **TGVs** (*trains à grande vitesse*), which nip along at 250 kph or more, are very useful for getting to Languedoc-Roussillon (see above). Unless you're in a hurry, however, the regular and regional trains (TER, T08 00 88 60 91, ter-sncf.com/languedoc €0.23 per min) are better for everyday travel: they are cheaper, will carry bicycles for free, and you don't have to book in advance. You can even avoid the queues by buying a ticket with your credit card from a machine in the station. These tickets are valid for two months, but like all train tickets in France you must make sure to date-stamp/validate (*composter*) your ticket in the station before boarding or you will be subject to a fine. Travel from Monday afternoons to Friday mornings (*période bleue*) is cheaper than weekends and holidays (*période blanche*). There are discounts for over 60s, under 26s and under 12s. Sometimes on less busy minor routes, SNCF buses run instead of trains.

TGVs run from Paris to Montpellier, from where there are frequent rail connections to Sète, Agde, Narbonne, Béziers, Carcasonne and Toulouse.

Trains link Carcassonne and Narbonne with Toulouse, and Narbonne with Perpignan, Béziers and Montpellier. A few services a day run from Carcassonne to Limoux, Couiza and Quillan (1 hr).

Road

Bicycle Although the French have great respect for cyclists, it's always best to avoid the busier roads. Check out route suggestions and maps on bikely.com and bikemap.net. In Montpellier you can hire and drop off a bike in one of 50 locations for €1 for four hours, or €2 for a day with Vélomagg. Elsewhere, rentals average €10-12 a day, more for a racing or mountain bike. **Mellow Velo** ① *T04 68 43 38 21*, *mellowvelos.com*, in Paraza on the Canal du Midi delivers bikes in the area. Local tourist offices can advise on other hire shops, alternatively check out holiday-bikes.com/fr.

Bus/coach Many bus servicesare geared towards getting kids to school, so hours are often early and buses run only once or twice a day. This is especially true in the Aude, , apart from the frequent buses that run in the environs of Carcassonne and from Narbonne to the beaches.

The Hérault has buses travelling the main routes four or five times a day from Montpellier or Béziers, but to complicate things many of the departures from Montpellier are from various outlying tramway stations (check departure points and schedules at herault-transport.fr). Services to Pézenas and the beaches (Palavas-les-Flots and La Grande Motte) are especially frequent in summer.

Car Motoring in Languedoc-Roussillon presents no great difficulties, although in summer the main *autoroute* that crosses the region (the A9) can get very busy, as it's also the main road between Spain and Italy.

Even minor roads in the mountains are well maintained, and most are well signposted, but a good map and/or a Sat Nav are essential. One wrong turn in the sprawl around the cities (especially Montpellier) can be fatal; signs are few and they never seem to be the ones you want. Driving in the city centres, with their traffic jams and one-way systems, can be frustrating, although here at least if you get lost, you can always follow the handy *Toutes directions* signs, which will eventually lead you out to a ring of roads around the city with many useful signs along the way. Parking garages cost €3-5 an hour.

It's always cheapest to fill up with petrol or diesel (*gazole*) at supermarkets, many of which now have 24-hour machines that take credit cards. Petrol stations of any kind are few and far between in the mountains.

Unless otherwise signposted, the speed limits on *autoroutes* is 130 kph. On two-lane D (departmental) roads it's 90 kph, and in towns (once you've passed the white sign announcing the town's name) it's 50 kph. Speeding fines start at €68 and can be as high as €4500 if you fail a breathalyzer test. If you have an accident, you will be asked to fill out a form called a *constat amiable*. If your French isn't up to it, wait for help rather than unwittingly incriminating yourself.

Car hire is almost always cheaper to arrange before you arrive, and it's essential you book in advance in the summer when cars can be in short supply. Look at the many car rental websites and then compare them to the fly/drive or rail/drive packages. You'll need to be at least 21 and have a credit card with the name of driver matching the name on the card. There may be supplemental charges for an extra driver or a child seat. Be sure to check the insurance and damage waiver before setting out, and always carry all the papers with you.

Where to stay in Languedoc: Carcassonne to Montpellier

When it comes to accommodation, Languedoc-Roussillon has a bit of everything, from sleek city hotels, designer B&Bs and converted castles to basic campsites in river gorges, shelters along Grande Randonnée (GR) long-distance paths and mountain huts. Gîtes, too, range across the spectrum, from simple studio apartments to luxurious historical conversions with all the frills, sleeping a dozen people or more.

Price codes

Where to stay

€€€€ over €200   €€€ €100-200

€€ €60-100   € under €60

Prices refer to the cost of two people sharing a double room in the high season.

Restaurants

€€€€ over €40   €€€ €30-40

€€ €20-30   € under €20

Prices refer to the average cost of a two-course meal for one person, with a drink and service and cover charge.

While prices in Languedoc-Roussillon are generally in line with the rest of France, in recent years the strict EU fire safety and health regulations have led to the closure of many of the old-fashioned hotels in small towns and rural areas. Prices in the survivors have inched up, and if you're touring, hotels for a night can be hard to find on spec, especially if you come in summer (when hotels are often full) or winter (when many close).

Stepping up to fill the gap, however, are a burgeoning number of *chambres d'hôtes* (bed and breakfasts), where a typical double room is priced roughly the same as a one-star hotel (€60-80). Breakfast isn't always included; if it's not, the average rate seems to be €10. Some top-range hotels charge as much as €30. Most of the hotels have restaurants and offer good-value breakfast/dinner packages, even for one night (*soirée étape*). Nearly all have at least one family room, and offer discounts or free stays for children. Out of high season it never hurts to ask for their best offer.

Prices also depend very much on where and when you go, whether your room has a view or a balcony, if it's situated at the back (usually quieter) or front of the hotel, what plumbing is on offer (en suite or not) and the newness of the fittings – many hotels and B&Bs charge a different price for every room. Prices in cities such as Carcassonne and Montpellier will be considerably more than elsewhere. That said, unless you go in peak season (July and August), you can often find special online offers on their websites. Outside of the ski areas, the cheapest times to visit are around November-March, although be aware that many hotels and B & Bs outside the cities close down completely.

Hotels

Hotels in France are graded from one to five stars according to their amenities. There are several umbrella organizations for hotels that guarantee certain standards – two of the best known are the middle-of-the-road Logis de France (generally two to three stars) and the very posh Relais & Châteaux (four or five stars, always connected to fine restaurants). The old one-star classic hotels with 20-second *minuteries* light timers on the stairs and in the halls, rock-hard sausage pillows, flowered wallpaper and toilets down the hall that made travelling in Languedoc a bit of an adventure are now becoming quite hard to find. That said, the sausage pillows still preside over many a rural hotel bed. Most rooms now have individual air conditioning, which can be essential in the summer months, and the majority offer free Wi-Fi, or at least internet that guests are welcome to use. Hotel parking garage fees start at €10 a night.

The main hotel discount websites such as lastminute.com, kayak.com or venere.com mostly concentrate on the chains. There are plenty of these (Kyriad, Campanile, Ibis,

Mercure, Formule1) in Languedoc-Roussillon, especially by the beaches, or in and around the cities or major *autoroute* junctions – all pleasant, and all pretty much the same, so we haven't included them in the text.

Most hotels have check-out times between 1100 and 1200. Most websites show pictures of the rooms, so you generally have an idea of what you're getting before you arrive. If you're arriving on spec, you may like to have a look at the room before committing.

Chambres d'hôtes (B&Bs)

If you like boutique hotels, Languedoc-Roussillon has a few, but there are far more boutique guesthouses and B&Bs. Many are located in old stone farmhouses (*mas*), *hôtels particuliers* or châteaux. Many are owned by good cooks who prepare convivial *table d'hôte* meals; some owners have impressive wine cellars and offer tastings; others have mini spas and offer courses and tours. Some will also collect you from the train station or airport. Many (because of French laws limiting B&Bs to five rooms) have self-catering apartments or a mix of rooms, suites, apartments and gîtes.

Because there's no reception or permanent staff, do make sure the owners know when to expect you. Also, don't hesitate to print out the maps on the websites – some are quite hard to find in the countryside (but are all the more peaceful and relaxing for it). Not all take credit cards, so be sure to ask when you book.

Farm stays

While not as well established as Italy's *agriturismo* industry, staying on farms is growing in popularity in Languedoc-Roussillon. Farms offer inexpensive accommodation and the chance to get back to nature at the same time. Some offer camping, others *chambres d'hôtes* and gîtes. Do check to see if they accept credit cards.

Camping

A large percentage of visitors, especially in July and August, camp or stay in mobile homes by the sea. The big sands are well equipped with campsites. If you want to shed all by the sea, Le Cap d'Agde has the largest naturist campsite in the world. Other popular (and decidedly more tranquil) campsites are along the rivers, set in the trees usually near swimming holes. Free camping (*camping sauvage*) is generally discouraged, and illegal in the national parks.

Campsites are graded like hotels from one to five stars, depending on the facilities on offer. Some have their own water parks, while others, sometimes municipally owned, are fairly basic. If you haven't brought your own, most will rent you a motorhome, caravan, bungalow or tent.

Gîtes d'étapes and refuges

Gîtes d'étapes are communal shelters set up along the GR long-distance paths, usually equipped with bunk beds in dorm rooms (bring your own sleeping bag) and basic kitchen facilities; you can pinpoint them at gite-etape.com. The mountain *refuges* in the Pyrenees are similar, but often serve meals; local tourist offices have phone numbers, as it's best to ring ahead to make sure there's space.

Self-catering

Outside of camping, this is often the cheapest option for a holiday, especially if you're travelling *en famille*. An increasingly popular option is the self-catering gîte as a part of a larger holiday complex (a hotel or swish B&B), which offers the best of both worlds – privacy and cooking facilities, but also the chance to enjoy all the added amenities, such as the spa, pool, restaurant, tennis courts, etc. The Jardins de St Benoît (see page 46) inland from Sigean in the Aude takes this to a whole new level in the region. Most rentals start on Saturday and in high season they are by the week; however, you can also find weekend rents or even cheaper weekday rentals, often with a minimum stay of two or three days.

For only slightly more than you'd typically pay to stay in a gîte, you can see a good swathe of Languedoc from a barge on the Canal du Midi or Canal Rhône-Sète (see page 86).

Booking

If you're coming to Languedoc in July and August, it's absolutely essential to book ahead, but it's a very good idea to do so at other times, too. You can book a wide range of accommodation and holiday packages (hotels, campsites, gîtes, farm holidays. B&Bs) directly through the official regional tourist board website en.sunfrance.com. They also have an impressive list of accommodation options for people with disabilities – Languedoc-Roussillon is proud to have more than any other region.

Otherwise, it's easiest to book directly through your accommodation's website. Many offer online or early-bird discounts, or packages combining meals, spa sessions and so on. Be sure to print out the confirmation in case there's any problem (they are usually very well run, but just in case), and then re-confirm by email or phone a day or two before to let them know your estimated time of arrival, especially if you're arriving at night. You'll usually be asked to give a credit card number for the first night to hold the booking.

Food and drink in Languedoc: Carcassonne to Montpellier

Centuries of poverty have kept Languedoc-Roussillon from developing into one of France's culinary regions, but today's chefs are well on track to change all that. It isn't surprising, as at their fingertips they have a palette of fresh ingredients to work with that few other regions in France can match – seafood and shellfish, bouquets of fragrant herbs, wild honeys, beef and lamb from the *causses*, flavour-packed fruit and vegetables ripened in the Mediterranean sun, goat cheeses from the Cévennes, wild mushrooms and truffles, duck and olives. Generalizations, though, are hard to make; because of the region's wildly varied geography and climates, each local area has its own specialities.

Regional specialities

In the **Hérault**, with its Bassin de Thau and fishing ports, seafood holds pride of place, with a variety of fish soups and stews, including Languedoc's version of *bouillabaisse* with ham and leeks, or Sète's *bourride*, a fish soup made from monkfish, anglerfish and/or cuttlefish. Sète is also famous for its *tielles* (pies filled with cuttlefish and onion) and mussels and baby octopus served on a spit. In Pézenas look for *petits pâtés de Pézenas* – little curried mutton pastries, said to have been introduced by the chef of the Viceroy of India. Olives are grown at the western end of the Hérault and in the Aude – the tiny *picholine* but also the larger, crescent-shaped green *lucques*, generally acclaimed as France's finest table olives. The signature dish of the **Aude** is cassoulet: a meltingly rich and flavoursome mélange of duck confits, pork, garlic, sausage (and sometimes lamb and even partridge) and Tarbais beans, baked in a clay pot for four to six hours in the oven. Castelnaudary, west of Carcassonne, claims to be the world capital of the dish.

Lying within the greatest southwestern France kingdom of duck, the Aude produces its own fine range of terrines, pâtés, maigrets, foie gras, and the ideal fat for making sautée potatoes. Limoux is known for its duck fricassée and some restaurants even have all-duck menus. There are truffles in winter too, at Villeneuve-Minervois.

Practicalities

Languedoc-Roussillon shuts down for lunch between 1200 and 1400, or even 1500 in many places. It's wise to get to your restaurant as soon as you can after 1200; to arrive much later, especially in rural areas, is to miss out on the *plat du jour* (dish of the day), or even risk being turned away. The dinner witching hour is from 1930 to 2030; if you're going to arrive later, be sure to tell the restaurant when you book. Throughout the guide, the days that restaurants are open for lunch and dinner have been indicated, and opening hours have been included when hours vary significantly from those listed above. In the cities, brasseries serve food throughout the day, at least in theory, although choices may well be limited outside classic French eating hours.

A bit confusingly, the French for menu is *carte*; the French use the word *menu* for a fixed priced meal, usually with several choices for the *entrée* (starter), *plat* (main course) and dessert. Generally a *menu* works out cheaper than ordering *à la carte*, and a lunch *menu* is nearly always better value than the dinner *menu*. A three-course lunch *formule* means little or no choice, but is cheapest of all. Some are under €10 and may even include a glass of wine (*vin compris*). Most restaurants offer at least one dinner menu under €30, although beware of the sometimes scandalous wine mark-ups.

A good many restaurants, including some of the best, are attached to hotels. In rural areas look for *ferme-auberges*, which are farms that prepare meals using their own meats and produce; some also offer packed lunches or snacks. In the bigger towns, bistrots and wine bars offer light evening meals or tapas.

Wine

Wine is the lifeblood of Languedoc-Roussillon. The region, an enormous patchwork of different types of rocky soils, exposures and microclimates – all the things that make up the French word *terroir* – is divided unevenly into 24 AOC (*Appellation d'Origine Contrôlée*) growing regions. Combine these AOC wines with the *Vins de Pays d'Oc* and *vins de table*, and it produces more wine than anywhere else in France. If you want to point a finger at the region responsible for Europe's wine lake, point here with both hands. In the past couple of decades, however, the wine has improved by leaps and bounds.

The wines of the Aude and Hérault have been well known for years. Minervois, elegant structured AOC wines named after the beautiful village of Minerve, was planted by Roman veterans and much appreciated back in Rome by Cicero. Powerful deep red Fitou, grown near Narbonne in the southern Corbières, was one of Louis XIV's favourites and is the region's oldest AOC (since 1948). of the big wine excitement in recent years has been concentrated in the *appellation* Côteaux du Languedoc, which extends from the Upper Hérault to Narbonne and Carcassonne. It's so vast that it has been subdivided into smaller zones such as Pic-St-Loup, Le Clape, Grès de Montpellier and the newest AOC area, Cabières. Coteaux du Languedoc also encompasses the well-established St-Chinian and its powerful neighbour Faugères, the most tannic of Languedoc's wines, grown since the early Middle Ages on sea-facing hills north of Béziers.

The rocky, arid Corbières, another vast region, has had its AOC credentials only since 1985 but has come on strong ever since. Subdivided into 11 *terroirs*, such as Boutenac, Lagrasse, Lézignan and Sigean, and producing full-bodied and spicy red wines (80%), they have also considerably improved in recent years, with an emphasis on bringing out the individual flavours and character of each area.

Although best known for red wines, most AOC areas also produce a percentage of whites. One of the classics is Picpoul de Pinet, literally 'lip stinger', an indigenous grape grown around Mèze and the Bassin de Thau, which goes well with seafood. Limoux produces the world's oldest bubbly – the Blanquette de Limoux. Along the coast of Hérault, Marseillan is the home of Noilly Prat, a white vermouth aged in barrels left in the sun (see page 76).

Most of all, quantity-wise, Languedoc produces *Vins de Pays d'Oc* (50% of all wine). These have less strict rules about the varieties of grapes that have to be used, and so have allowed some winemakers to experiment and create genuine marvels. One of the best ways to learn more (short of drinking your way through every label) is to attend a regional wine-tasting class – something that has become increasingly popular in recent years.

Festivals in Languedoc: Carcassonne to Montpellier

Languedoc-Roussillon loves a party and puts on a full calendar of festivities and events. A select few are listed below, but to include them all would take up all the pages of this book.

Prestigious ballet, music, theatre and film festivals take place in the cities year round, especially in Montpellier. Elsewhere, age-old traditions have survived more or less intact, and where they haven't, the locals love to put on jousts, troubadour singsongs and other events dedicated to evoking the good old pre-Simon de Montfort days. In summer, juices flow at outdoor music festivals and in two major events that in France are unique to the region: the summer ferias, with their bulls, music, bodegas and general merriment, and the nautical jousts or *joutes nautiques* (see page 77). Do check the websites or tourist offices for exact dates and times; increasingly you can also buy tickets online before you go.

January
Carnival: Los Fecos *Limoux, T04 68 31 35 09, limoux.fr.* Los Fecos goes back four centuries and features 24 town guilds, each with their own costumes, who take turns parading at weekends in Place de la République from mid-January to mid-March (it's the longest running festival in France). There's music, joking and satirizing in Occitan – and drinking of Blanquette.

Fête du Cochon *St-Pons-de-Thomières, T04 67 97 39 39, saint-pons-tourisme.com.* Feast on freshly roasted pork, *saucisse* and other pork produce.

Fête du Mimosa *Roquebrun, T04 67 89 79 97, roquebrun.org.* Carnival of flowers, with floats and crafts.

Le Poulain *Pézenas, T04 67 98 36 40, ot-pezenas-valdherault.com.* Traditional carnival and procession, featuring a parade with a giant mock colt. It has been the town's totem beast since 1226, when a foal was born here to the favourite mare of Louis VIII.

Festival a 100%, *Montpellier, T09 81 89 51 12, festival100pour100.com.* Edgy, urban world 100% eclectic music festival, with films and exhibitions

March
Toques et Clochers, *near Limoux, T04 68 31 11 82, sieurdarques.com.* Sponsored by the Sieur d'Arques winery, this popular wine tasting and wine auction (led by one of France's top chefs) supports the restoration of a local belltower (clocher); good food and art too. It takes place in a different AOC Limoux village every year

April
Escale à Sete, *Sète, T04 67 46 07 14, ot-sete. fr.* Four days festival celebrating traditional sailing ships and maritime traditions.

May,

Cavalcade *Pézenas, T04 67 98 36 40, ot-pezenas-valdherault.com.* Celebration of the town's glory days, with a procession in historic costumes, a handicraft market and more.

June
Festival de Maguelone *Cathédrale de Maguelone, Palavas, T04 67 60 69 92, musiqueancienneamaguelone.com.* Two weeks of medieval, Renaissance and baroque music.

Le Printemps des Comédiens *Montpellier, T04 67 63 66 67, printempsdescomediens.com.* The venue is the Château d'O, for the biggest theatre and performing arts festival in France after Avignon.

Montpellier Danse *Montpellier, T08 00 60 07 40, montpellierdanse.com.* Performances by over 20 ballet companies, from mid-June to early July.

July
Festival de Radio France *Montpellier, T04 67 02 02 01, festivalradiofrancemontpellier.com.* Classical, jazz, chamber music, electronic, reggae, etc. Concerts, including many free events, mostly take place in the Corum.

Festival des 2 Cités *Carcassonne, T04 68 11 59 15, festivaldecarcassonne.com.* The two Carcassonnes (upper and lower) celebrate with pop, opera, jazz and orchestral concerts of all kinds. There's a spectacular fireworks display on 14 July.

Bastille Day *Narbonne, festivalnarbonne.org.* Four days of celebrations and fireworks.

Festival Jazz à Sète *Théâtre de la Mer, T08 92 68 36 22, jazzasete.com.* Not only jazz, but flamenco, blues and soul, this festival attracts headline performers such as Jeff Beck to Sète's seaside theatre during the second week of July.

Festival de Thau *Mèze, Frontigan and Gigeac, T04 67 43 93 08, festivaldethau.com.* World and alternative music festival that keeps the baby oysters up late for three weeks in July.

Festival de Lamalou *Théâtre du Casino, Lamalou-les-Bains, T04 67 95 67 35, festivaldelamalou.com.* Summer festival of operettas and music theatre (mostly French, but also *Hello Dolly!* and *Carmen*) takes place for six weeks in July and August in the spa's bijou theatre dating from 1878. See also December.

August
Fiest'a Sète *Sète, T04 67 74 48 44, fiestasete.com.* Some of the greatest musicians from Cuba, Africa, Brazil and the Caribbean perform in Sète during the first week of August.

Feria de Béziers *Arènes de Béziers, T04 67 76 13 45, arenes-de-beziers.com.* Taking place over four days around 15 August, Bézier's feria is the single biggest event in Languedoc-Roussillon, drawing over one million people. *Corridas* in the Arènes, concerts, bodegas, street festivals and parties.

October
Fête de la Châtaigne *St-Pons-de-Thomières, T04 67 97 39 39, saint-pons-tourisme.com.* Late October fête dedicated to chestnuts in all their glory.

Festival International du Cinéma Méditerranéen *Montpellier, T04 67 58 43 47, cinemed.tm.fr.* Takes place the last week in October and is dedicated to documentaries, shorts and independent films from around the Mediterranean.

November
Fête du Marron d'Olargues et du Vin Nouveau *Orlargues, T04 67 97 71 76, olargues.org.* Festival of chestnuts and *vin primeur*.

December
Festival de Lamalou *Théâtre du Casino, Lamalou-les-Bains, T04 67 95 67 35, festivaldelamalou.com.* Winter festival of operettas and music theatre.

Marchés de Noël Christmas markets throughout the region, notably in Pézenas, Carcassonne and Montpellier.

Essentials A-Z

Customs and immigration
UK and EU visitors need a valid passport
to enter France. Standard tourist visas for
non-EU visitors are valid for 90 days and
encompass the whole EU zone.

Disabled travellers
Languedoc-Roussillon claims to be top
when it comes to accommodating visitors
with special needs; at en.sunfrance.com
you can download a complete list of gîtes,
campsites, restaurants, parks, sites and
activities adapted for people with a range
of disabilities. Most trains, and Montpellier's
trams, are wheelchair-friendly, or ring
for a **Taxi Tram** (T04 67 92 04 98) which
provides transport in the city and beyond,
as does the region-wide **Ulysse Transport**
(ulysse-transport.fr). Alternatively, hire your
own adapted transport with **Holiday Cars**
(T04 78 60 31 31, holiday-cars.biz). When
booking hotel rooms, be sure to ask for a
une chambre adaptée.

Emergencies
European emergency line T112. **Fire
service** T18. **Police** T17. **SAMU** (medical
emergencies) T15.

Etiquette
The French are very polite. Greet everyone
in shops, restaurants and hotels, with a
"Bonjour, Madame/Mademoiselle/Monsieur"
and then an *"Au revoir"* when you depart.
They also love to make *les bises* (cheek air
kisses) even when first introduced if at least
one member of the party is female (man-to-
man, a handshake will do).

Families
Languedoc-Roussillon is a great destination
for family holidays; people here are fond of
children, and there are long sandy beaches
and endless things for them to do. Most

restaurants offer a *menu enfant* (usually *steak
frites*). High chairs are rarer, but hotels often
have family rooms and cots.

Health
Comprehensive travel and medical
insurance is recommended. EU citizens
should apply for a free European Health
Insurance Card or EHIC (ehic.org.uk),
which entitles you to emergency medical
treatment on the same terms as French
nationals. Note that you will have to pay all
charges and prescriptions up front and be
reimbursed either through a local CPAM
office (Caisse Primaire D'Assurance Maladie)
in France or once you return home. If you
develop a minor ailment while on holiday,
a visit to any pharmacy will allow you to
discuss your concerns with highly qualified
staff, who can give medical advice and
recommend treatment. Outside normal
opening hours, the address of the nearest
duty pharmacy (*pharmacie de garde*) is
displayed in the pharmacy window.

The out-of-hours number for a local
doctor (*médecin généraliste*) may also be
listed. In a serious emergency, go to the
accident and emergency department
(*urgences*) at the nearest Centre Hospitalier
(numbers listed in the Essentials section
at the beginning of each chapter) or call
an ambulance (SAMU) by dialling T15, or
T18 (the firemen) in rural areas, as they are
trained for emergencies and may well arrive
faster.

Insurance
Comprehensive travel and medical
insurance is strongly recommended, as the
European Health Insurance Card (EHIC) does
not cover medical repatriation, ongoing
medical treatment or treatment considered
to be non-urgent. Check for exclusions if
you mean to engage in risky sports. Keep all

insurance documents to hand; a good way to keep track of your policies is to email the details to yourself.

Make sure you have adequate insurance when hiring a car and always ask how much excess you are liable for if the vehicle is returned with any damage. It is generally worth paying a little more for a collision damage waiver. If driving your own vehicle to France, contact your insurers before you travel to ensure you are adequately covered, and keep the documents in your vehicle in case you need to prove it.

Money

The French currency is the euro (€). There are ATM machines in every town, and nearly all hotels, restaurants and shops accept credit cards, although beware that many B&Bs do not. Note that many North American cards lack a chip necessary for them to work in toll machines, train ticket machines or in 24-hour petrol stations, so check with your bank before you leave. It's also worth asking your bank for information on how to save money on cash withdrawal charges. It's very difficult these days to find a French bank to change currency or traveller's cheques; try at the airport exchanges or main post offices in big cities.

Languedoc isn't as expensive as many parts of France, although admission prices have gone up recently. Excluding accommodation costs, you'll need to budget about €50 per person a day for meals, transport and entrance fees.

Many cities and *départements* offer discount passes; usually you pay full whack at the first attraction, then save money by presenting your pass at other participating sights. Senior citizens, students (bring ID) and children nearly always pay less as well, or go free. Some places offer special rates for families – it's worth asking.

Opening hours

In general, museums (and many shops) close on Mondays, and most close for lunch. Sights tend to stay open continuously in July and August, but close for lunch in spring and autumn; by winter opening hours are often curtailed to weekends, national holidays and French school half-term breaks. The more out of season, the more advisable it is to ring ahead to make sure someone's there. Churches often close between 1200 and 1500.

Police

There are two types of police in France. The Police Municipal handle mostly traffic issues in cities; the Gendarmes take care of everything else. Note that in France you can legally be stopped for ID checks for no reason (usually for belonging to a minority or looking scruffy). If your passport or any other valuables are lost and stolen, visit the *gendarmerie* (police station) for the necessary paperwork.

Post

La Poste is reliable, but recently many rural bureaux have been closed down, or replaced by a counter in shops. Most newsagents and *tabacs* sell stamps (*timbres*) for postcards and letters to Europe but hardly ever for other destinations. Post offices are closed Saturday afternoons and Sundays, and usually for lunch, too.

Safety

Violent crime is rare in France, but there's a healthy amount of petty theft in Montpellier; you should avoid some of the run-down quarters after dark. Just be as sensible as you are at home, and don't leave tempting items visible in your car, insure your camera and don't carry all your money with you in one place.

Telephone

The French have dispensed with area codes, and all numbers dialled within the country are now 10 digits. If a number begins with 06 it's a mobile phone. The country code is 33; when dialling from abroad, leave out the first 0 (T+332). Directory assistance, T118 218.

Time difference

One hour ahead of GMT; six hours ahead of EST.

Tipping

French bar and restaurant bills nearly always include a 15% service charge so tipping a little extra is discretionary. Taxi drivers appreciate it if you round up the fare or add an extra couple of euros for any help with your bags. Give a guide a euro or two at the end of guided tours.

Tourist information

Every town of any size will have a tourist information office, and nearly always someone there will speak English. They all have a web presence, although it may only be in French.

Tourist offices

Languedoc Regional Tourism Board
L'Acropole, 954, avenue Jean Mermoz, 34960 Montpellier, T04 67 20 02 20, en.sunfrance.com.

Hérault Tourist Board *Avenue des Moulins, 34184 Montpellier, T04 67 67 71 71, herault-tourisme.com.*

Aude Tourist Board *Allée Raymond Courrière, 11855 Carcassonne, T04 68 11 66 00, audetourisme.com.*

Useful websites

Among other useful websites covering a range of topics are languedoc-france. info, creme-de-languedoc.com and languedocsun.com. The region's official website, en.sunfrance.com, is chock-full of useful information and it offers packages and online reservations, as well as information about events and exhibitions.

Voltage

The electrical current in France is 220 volts 50 Hz; Plugs are the standard European round two-pin variety.

Contents

Footprint features

Aude

Now that heresy no longer brings down armies, the Aude proudly bills itself 'Le Pays Cathare'. Carcassonne, the city with the fairytale citadel, is the capital, while just to the south, in the rugged Corbières, rocky spurs are crowned with vertiginous castles where the last of the Cathars sought refuge from Simon de Montfort. Equally unorthodox Rennes-le-Château is here as well – not a place the tourist board actively promotes, but a must-see for fans of *Holy Blood, Holy Grail* and *The Da Vinci Code*.

And there's more. Down by the Mediterranean, Narbonne, the capital of Roman Languedoc, became the religious centre of the region in the Middle Ages. It has for a stunning centrepiece a towering Gothic complex, including the cathedral and episcopal palace; the latter is now home to two excellent museums. The once-powerful abbey of Fontfroide is a short drive away, as are long sandy beaches, and at Sigean you can visit the elephants, lions and giraffes wandering freely in the immense African Reserve. The Aude has a long stretch of the idyllic Canal du Midi, but most of all it has wine: Corbières, part of Minervois (which it shares with Hérault), bubbly Blanquette de Limoux, Fitou and Le Clape.

Carcassonne and around

The Aude's capital has three distinct parts. Down by the river there's the modern city that surrounds the tight-knit medieval 'new town', the Bastide St Louis; at the top is the outrageously picturesque prize, the Cité of Carcassonne. In a tiara of witch-hatted towers, the Cité is the perfect storybook citadel and since 1997 it has been a World Heritage Site.

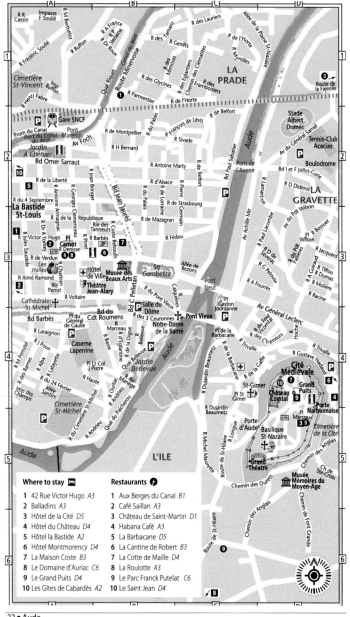

Where to stay 🛏

1 42 Rue Victor Hugo *A3*
2 Balladins *A3*
3 Hôtel de la Cité *D5*
4 Hôtel du Château *D4*
5 Hôtel la Bastide *A2*
6 Hôtel Montmorency *D4*
7 La Maison Coste *B3*
8 Le Domaine d'Auriac *C6*
9 Le Grand Puits *D4*
10 Les Gîtes de Cabardès *A2*

Restaurants 🍴

1 Aux Berges du Canal *B1*
2 Café Saillan *A3*
3 Château de Saint-Martin *D1*
4 Habana Café *A3*
5 La Barbacane *D5*
6 La Cantine de Robert *B3*
7 La Cotte de Maille *D4*
8 La Roulotte *A3*
9 Le Parc Franck Putelat *C6*
10 Le Saint Jean *D4*

Cité de Carcassonne

Built at a strategic bend in the Aude, the site has been occupied since the eighth century BC. The Gauls, Romans, Visigoths, Arabs and Franks were here, followed in the 11th century by the Trencavels – the Viscounts of Carcassonne, Albi, Béziers and Nîmes, powerful allies of the Counts of Toulouse.

When Innocent III declared the Albigensian Crusade, the young Viscount Raymond-Roger Trencavel gallantly offered to shelter all the 'persecuted people' of the south. The Roman walls were still good enough to keep the Crusaders at bay for two weeks, so they resorted to trickery, luring Trencavel outside the walls and throwing him in prison. Soon after, he was found dead – poisoned, it was rumoured. Blame fell on Simon de Montfort, who declared himself count of all his lands, which his son later ceded to the French crown.

Louis XI (St Louis) and his son Philippe III made Carcassonne the seat of French power in Languedoc, building the greatest and most impregnable citadel in Europe. Never attacked, it became obsolete with the Treaty of the Pyrenees in 1659 and slowly fell into ruin, and there were moves to quarry its stone for new buildings in the Ville Basse. Novelist Prosper Mérimée, Inspector-General of Historic Monuments, raised the alarm, and in 1853 Eugène Viollet-le-Duc, restorer of Notre-Dame in Paris, came to the rescue and rebuilt it as it should have looked all along.

Porte Narbonnaise and Les Lices

The Cité has four gates, but only the Porte Narbonnaise was (and still is) accessible by road. As powerful as it looks, with its two portcullises and towers, it is militarily the weakest point in the defences. Between the two curtains of walls (the outer ones were built by Louis IX, the inner ones date back to Roman times) runs a broad open space, Les Lices, where the knights would train and hold their jousts. You can walk around the walls or take a guided tour in one of the horse-drawn carriages by the gate.

Château Comtal and ramparts

ⓘ *1 rue Viollet-le-Duc, T04 68 11 70 70, carcassonne.monuments-nationaux.fr. Apr-Sep daily 0930-1830, Oct-Mar daily 0930-1700. €8.50, €5 young person (18-25), under 18s and EU citizens under 26 free. Guided tours of various lengths €8.50-13. Note that the ticket office closes 30 mins before the castle.*

This castle was built on Roman foundations by the Trencavels. The impressive outer walls and barbican had to be added when it became residence of the French seneschal, to protect him from the angry populace. Today, it houses models, sculptures and inscriptions dating back to Roman times, Merovingian tombs and 14th-century alabasters and altarpieces salvaged from destroyed churches in the countryside. There's a special exhibition on the restoration, including Viollet-le-Duc's drawings, plans and photos, paintings of what the Cité looked like before he arrived and audiovisuals and interactive displays. You can walk around most of the 3 km of walls with their 52 towers, and either hire an audio guide or join one of the free 45-minute guided tours in French.

Near the château, a little square has a massive well called the **Grand Puits**, the largest of the Cité's 22 wells. Legend has it that the Visigoths hid the Treasure of Solomon here when they heard Attila the Hun was coming; if anyone ever found it, they're not telling.

Basilique St-Nazaire

ⓘ *Place de l'Eglise. Apr-Sep Mon-Sat 0900-1145 and 1345-1800, Sun 0900-1045 and 1400-1700, Oct-Mar Mon-Sat 0900-1145 and 1345-1700, Sun 0900-1045 and 1400-1630.*

Pope Urban V was visiting Carcassonne when he ordered the construction of this church in 1096. It started off Romanesque, until the northerners moved in and made it into a tall Gothic hybrid with a pair of enormous rose windows and projecting gargoyles. The organ is the biggest in the south of France. A plaque marks the tomb of Simon de Montfort, who was killed in 1218 while besieging Toulouse, but his relatives transferred his body to a safer resting spot in the north in 1224.

Musée Mémoires du Moyen-Age

ⓘ *40 Chemin des Anglais, T04 68 71 08 65, mmma.chez.com. Daily 1000-1900, closed at Christmas. €5, €4 students; €3 child.*
This is fun for the kids – models, videos and son et lumière evoke the Middle Ages and medieval siege machinery.

La Ville Basse: the Bastide St-Louis

The Cité has 120 inhabitants; the other 45,400 Carcassonnais live and work in the lower city. Its slightly claustrophobic core is the Bastide St-Louis, a medieval 'new town' founded by St Louis in 1247, after the inhabitants (who used to live just outside the walls of the Cité) tried to help the son of Raymond-Roger Trencavel recapture his castle. Louis knocked their houses down and moved them here. Like all *bastides*, the streets were laid out in a grid around a square – in this case, pretty **Place Carnot**. The square has a marble Fontaine de Neptune (1770) and a market that takes place on Tuesday, Thursday and Saturday mornings. In winter part of the square is iced over for skaters.

Le Pont Vieux

Built in the 14th century, this bridge, carried on twelve arches, is still in business; its tiny Gothic chapel of Notre Dame de la Santé (1538) is all that remains of a medieval hospital.

Musée des Beaux-Arts

ⓘ *1 rue de Verdun, T04 68 77 73 70. 15 Sep-15 Jun Tue-Sat 1000-1200 and 1400-1800; 15 Jun-15 Sep daily 1000-1800, closed holidays. Free.*
This museum of mostly French works from the 17th to 20th centuries has works by Rigaud, Corot, Chardin (a charming still-life, **The Kitchen Table**), Courbet, local painter Jacques Gamelin and a collection of ceramics.

Around Carcassonne

Châteaux de Lastours

ⓘ *Lastours, 16 km north of Carcassonne, T04 68 77 56 02, les4chateaux-lastours.lwdsoftware. net. Feb, Mar, mid-Nov to Dec Sat-Sun and national holidays 1000-1700, Apr-Jun and Sep daily 1000-1800, Jul-Aug daily 0900-2000, Oct to mid-Nov daily 1000-1700. €5, €2 child.*
There are actually four castles spread out dramatically across a ridge in the Cabardès, a ruggedly austere area of ancient iron and gold mines. The lords of the oldest castles, Cabaret, Surdespine and Quertinheux, were Cathars and famous patrons of the arts, and stood up to Simon de Montfort's attack in 1211. Cabaret later became the centre of a Cathar resistance movement until finally surrendering in 1229. In 1240, the king rebuilt the castles and added the fourth, the Tour Régine. The visit includes ruins of the medieval village of Cabaret and views from the **Belvedere de Montfermier**.

South of Carcassonne

From Carcassonne the D118 follows the Aude up into a relatively sleepy but pretty corner of Languedoc to **Limoux**, an attractive town on the river, famous for its sparkling Blanquette de Limoux wine and for its equally effervescent winter festival, the Fécos. It's a long, narrow town that was once enclosed in ramparts, with a 14th-century bridge, the **Pont Neuf**, and a lovely arcaded **Place de la République** and fountain in the shadow of the Gothic steeple of **St Martin**.

Besides tasting the local bubbly, visit the **Musée Petiet** ① *Promenade du Tivoli, T04 68 31 85 03, Sep-Jun Wed-Fri 0900-1200 and 1400-1800 (in Jun & Sep also open Tue) Sat 1000-1200 and 1400-1700, Jul-Aug Tue-Sun 0900-1900*, next to Limoux's tourist office. This is in the atmospheric late 19th-century home and *atelier* of the Petiet family of artists, one of whom, Marie (1854-1893), painted intimate domestic scenes (*Les Blanchisseuses*, 1882). Her works are the star attractions, along with landscapes by the Aude's own pointillist, Achille Laugé.

Just north of Limoux, off the D118, the **Jardin aux Plantes parfumées la Bouichère** ① *T04 68 31 49 94, labouichere.com, May-early Oct Wed-Sun 1300-1800, mid-Jun to mid-Aug Wed-Sun 1000-1800, €6.90, €3.90 child*, was planted 20 years ago by Gabrielle and Pierre Gerber. They created a 2-ha oasis with 2500 fragrant trees, plants and flowers, made all the more striking for the sprawl that has grown around them. Parrots and a pair of donkeys call it home.

Although they hate to admit it in France's great champagne cellars, the truth is that their world-famous bubbly is the copycat. The first fizzy wine was invented here in 1531, when a wine-making monk at the **Abbaye de St-Hilaire** accidentally discovered the technique for making it fizz – a method known as Blanquette Méthode Ancestrale, made solely of *mauzac* and bottled during the waning moon of March. The **abbey** ① *12 km northeast of Limoux, T04 68 69 62 76, abbayedesainthilaire.pagesperso-orange.fr Apr-Jun, Sep-Oct daily 1000-1200 and 1400-1800, Jul-Aug daily 1000-1900, Nov-Mar 1000-1200 and 1400-1700, closed Christmas holidays, €4, €2 children*) has a magnificent 12th-century sarcophagus depicting the life of St Sernin of Toulouse by the Master of Cabestany, and a charming 14th-century cloister and Capitulary with a 16th-century painted ceiling. In the refectory, don't miss the lectern hollowed out of a pillar, so the dining monks could listen to a reader without seeing him.

South of Limoux, **Alet-les-Bains** is a pretty medieval hamlet snoozing alongside the Aude, with a thermal pool and free mineral water from the public taps, which is said to be good for the digestion. It's hard to believe, but its **Abbaye Notre-Dame d'Alet** ① *mid-Feb to Dec Mon-Sat 1000-1200 and 1430-1800, €3*, was once the seat of a powerful bishop, who expanded a Carolingian abbey church into a cathedral in 1318. The Protestants left it a picturesque ruin.

Carcassonne and around listings

For Sleeping and Eating price codes and other relevant information, see page 10.

🛏 Where to stay

Carcassonne and around *p21*

€€€€ Hôtel de la Cité, *Place Auguste-Pierre Pont, T04 68 71 98 71, hoteldelacite.com.* In the heart of the Cité, these 40 sumptuous rooms and 21 suites in the former bishop's palace have hosted everyone from Queen Elizabeth to Walt Disney. Expect bags of medieval atmosphere and luxury amid oak beams, marble baths, spiral stairs, secret terraces, heated pool and gardens and a gorgeous library/bar. Kids under 16 can stay for free in their parents' room.

€€€€ Le Domaine d'Auriac, *Rte de St-Hilaire, T04 68 25 72 22, domaine-d-auriac. com.* Far from the crowds but only 7 km from Carcassonne airport, this manor house hotel has 24 rooms lavishly decorated in flowery patterns. The hotel sits on a 70-ha estate of woods and vines, with a large outdoor pool, tennis court, an 18-hole golf course and a fine restaurant serving traditional cuisine with tables by the roaring fire in winter, or alfresco in the garden in summer.

€€€ 42 Rue Victor Hugo, *42 rue Victor Hugo, T09 77 52 44 36, 42ruevictorhugo.com.* Just off Place Carnot in the Bastide St-Louis, this elegant B&B in an 18th-century *hôtel particulier* is perfect for couples. There are two apartments and a master bedroom, sleekly designed in shades of grey, all with superbly decadent showers and exquisite cotton sheets. Owners Peter and Debrah are exceptionally helpful and knowledgeable, and Peter is an excellent chef. Minimum stay is two nights, and there are special weekend offers.

€€€ Hôtel du Château, *2 rue Camille St-Saens, T04 68 11 38 38, hotel-du-chateau.net.* This cushy little 16-room hotel is located just outside the Cité. Rooms are stylish and

cosy, equipped with flat-screen TVs, air conditioning and CD players. The attractive grounds under the medieval walls offer a heated pool (Easter-November) and year-round jacuzzi. The hotel has no restaurant, but there's a bar and the breakfast (€12) is copious.

€€ Hôtel la Bastide, *81 rue de la Liberté, T04 68 71 96 89, hotel-bastide.fr.* This pleasant 28-room hotel makes a nice change from the cookie-cutter chain hotels in the same price range. It doesn't have a restaurant, but it has everything else you need: friendly owners, air conditioning, flat-screen TVs, internet, breakfast (€7) and a private garage. Prices are at the bottom of this range.

€€ Hôtel Montmorency, *9 rue Camille St-Saens, T04 68 11 96 70, lemontmorency.com.* Just a few minutes from the Cité, this stylish hotel offers 20 quiet, air-conditioned if rather small rooms. There's a garden patio, and guests can also make use of the heated pool and jacuzzi at the nearby Hôtel du Château, which has the same owners. Free parking, and computers in the lobby.

€€ La Maison Coste, *40 rue Coste Rebouhl, T04 68 77 12 15, maison-coste.com.* The charming owners of this B&B, Manu and Michel, run an interior design boutique so everything in the three spacious rooms and two suites is in immaculate taste. There's a Jacuzzi, small garden and a tea room but no TV or phones, so peace and quiet guaranteed. Hearty continental breakfast included.

€ Balladins, *3 allée Gilles de Roberval, T04 68 71 99 50, etoilecarcassonne.fr.* Although located by the airport in an industrial zone, this immaculate, modern, family-run hotel is very popular with budget travellers. Red, white and black prevail in the public rooms and 38 bedrooms, and there's a good restaurant, too.

€ Le Grand Puits, *8 place du Grand Puits, T04 68 25 16 67, legrandpuits.free.fr.* Situated in the Cité, book early to stay in one of these three rooms with wood-beam ceilings. The blue room sleeps four and comes with a patio and kitchenette; the orange room sleeps five and has a kitchenette and beautiful views over the Montagne Noir; the yellow room sleeps two and has all you need to make your own continental breakfast.

Self-catering
Les Gîtes de Cabardès, *7 rue des Jardins, Ventenac-Cabardès, T04 68 24 08 23, carcassonne-holidays.com.* On the edge of a village only 10 minutes from Carcassonne, these are three modern and very well-equipped gîtes that sleep up to six people and share a pool. A week out of season starts at €260 for two.

Restaurants

Carcassonne and around *p21*
€€€€ La Barbacane, *Place Auguste-Pierre Pont, T04 68 71 98 71, hoteldelacite.com. Thu-Mon for dinner.* The Hotel de la Cité's restaurant offers fabulous dining in a hall where the viscounts would have felt at home. The food lives up to the setting; classics include Charolais beef with foie gras, and sole glazed in champagne. There are exquisite vegetarian options, home-made bread, and masterpieces prepared by the special pastry chef, including a modern take on crêpes Suzette. Reservations required. The hotel's brasserie, **Le Donjon**, and summer garden restaurant, Le Jardin de l'Evêque (Jun-Sep) are also excellent and less pricey.
€€€€ Le Parc Franck Putelat, *Chemin des Anglais, T04 68 71 80 80, restaurantleparcfranckputelat.fr. Tue-Sat for lunch and dinner.* Young Franck Putelat, one of the stars of France's culinary firmament, runs this laid-back, quirky and stylish restaurant in a garden at the foot of the Cité. Menus feature a mix of classics (truffled Bresse chicken) and innovations (roast scallops with savoy cabbage, Morteau

sausage and juniper) that have won him accolades from even the snootiest critics. Set-price weekday lunch with a glass of wine and coffee is €31, or let him follow his fancy for €118 a head. Book in advance.
€€€ Château de St-Martin, *Hameau de Montredon (3 km from Carcassonne) T04 68 71 09 53, chateausaintmartin.net. Apr-Sep Thu-Tue for lunch and dinner, Oct-Mar Mon-Tue, Thu-Sat for lunch and dinner, Sun for lunch.* No one makes cassoulet better than chef Jean-Claude, and it can be slowly savoured either in the garden or in the atmospheric 12th-century tower. He also specializes in seafood. It may not be easy, but try to save a bit of room for the lovely desserts. Menus from €33-57.
€€ Aux Berges du Canal, *48 rte Minervoise, T04 68 26 60 15, auxbergesducanal.pagesperso-orange.fr. Thu-Tue for lunch and dinner.* On the banks of the Canal du Midi, this unpretentious little family-run restaurant offers a varied menu, including fish, beef and lamb dishes, as well as a cassoulet. Good value for money; menus start at €16.
€€ La Cantine de Robert, *Place de Lattre de Tassigny, T04 68 47 37 80, restaurantrobertrodriguez.com. Mon-Sat lunch. Mon-Wed and Thu-Sat dinner.* Robert Rodriguez's 1930s-style bistro is opposite his far pricier headquarters, L'Atelier. It offers an affordable chance to taste well-prepared southern French classics from *daube* to platters of cheese and charcuterie, all with a superb choice of wines. Book.
€€ La Cotte de Maille, *2 rue St-Jean, T04 68 72 36 24, cottedemailles.com. Jul-Sep daily for lunch and dinner, Oct-Mar Fri-Wed for lunch and dinner.* This candlelit restaurant offers a chance for total sensory medieval immersion. Chef Claudine serves medieval cuisine in filling portions, from the original cassoulet de Carcassonne cooked with lamb (instead of duck) and beef with salsify, to parsnips and Jerusalem artichokes and game dishes. All can be washed down with *hypocras* (spicy wine) or *moretum* (medieval sangria).

€ La Roulotte, *6 rue Denisse, T04 68 25 07 03. Tue-Sat for lunch and dinner.* This welcoming little restaurant (a *roulotte* is a gypsy caravan) off Place Carnot is great for a romantic evening, but also fine for kids – they even supply crayons. The furnishings come from antique shops and flea markets, and you can dine alfresco in good weather. The menu is small and changes according to the market, but the food is fresh and refined.

€ Le Saint Jean, *1 place St Jean, T04 68 47 42 43, le-saint-jean.fr. Jun-Sep daily 0900-2200, Oct-May Wed-Mon 0900-2200.* The terrace overlooking Viollet-le-Duc's pointy-roofed towers is an oasis of calm in the Cité, but that's not the only reason to stop here. The duck and cassoulet are tasty, and there are a selection of fresh *salades composées*, including the 'Visigoth' with four kinds of cheese. In July and August there's often live jazz or salsa, when the bar stays open late. They also do breakfast. Lunch menus from €11.

Cafés and bars

Café Saillan, *31 rue du Dr Tomey, T04 68 71 39 96. Open Tue-Sat 0700-0200.* In the same family for three generations, this extremely popular café has had an arty overhaul and stays open late; live music some weekends.

Habana Café, *23 Place Carnot, T04 68 71 28 78 Open daily 0900-0200.* Best spot in town for a mojito, with a big terrace for hangout out late at night.

⊕ Entertainment

Carcassonne and around *p21*
Clubs

Black Bottom, *Rte de Limoux, T04 68 47 37 11. Thu-Sat 2200-0500.* Four kilometres south of Carcassonne, this is a classic disco of long standing.

La Bulle, *115 rue Barbacane, T04 68 72 47 70, labulle-carcassonne.fr. Thu-Sat 2200-0500.* The DJs keep a young crowd on their feet playing House and techno hits.

Le Conti, *16 rue de l'Aigle-d'Or, T04 68 25 39 40. Thu-Sat 2200-0500.* The after-hours bar and disco in the lower town, attracting a mostly 20-something crowd. They often put on Latin nights.

⊕ Festivals

Le Chevalier de la Foi, *Les Lices de la Cité, ring the tourist office for times: T04 68 10 24 30. Every afternoon in Jul and Aug.* A bravura display of jousting, costumes and storytelling, in which Simon de Montfort's crew satisfyingly lose.

○ Shopping

Carcassonne and around *p21*
Art

La Maison du Chevalier, *56 rue Trivalle, T04 68 47 36 36, maisonduchevalier.com. Apr-Sep Mon-Sat 1030-1200 and 1330-1830, Oct-Mar ring ahead.* On the road to the Cité, a sleek gallery of contemporary art, sculpture and photography.

Clothes and accessories

La Maison du Sud, *15 rue Porte d'Aude, T04 68 47 10 06. Open 1000-2000.* Most of the many souvenir shops in the Cité are much of a muchness – this one has a touch of class and sells handsome straw hats, soaps and cotton and linen shirts.

Lauranne de France, *11 rue St Louis, T04 68 71 89 10. Jul-Aug 0900-2130, Sep-Jun 0930-2000.* Handmade lace in all its forms.

Crafts

Le Vieux Lavoir/Coopérative Artisanale de la Cité, *11 rue du Plô, T04 68 71 00 04. levieuxlavoir.canalblog.com. Jul-Aug 1000-2000, shorter hours the rest of the year.* Items made by craft workers from across Languedoc.

Food and drink

Cabanel, *72 allées d'Iéna, T04 68 25 02 58. Mon-Sat 0800-1200 and 1400-1900.* Cabanel's distillery and boutique offers boozy treats you won't find elsewhere: herbal liqueurs, their own pastis, and a fifth-century aperitif called Micheline, as well as a wide choice of wines.

La Ferme, *55 rue Verdun, T04 68 25 02 15 . Tue-Fri 0800-1230 and 1500-1930, Sat 0700-1300 and 1500-1930.* Upmarket food shop that stocks 6000 different products, ranging from fine artisinal cheeses and charcuterie to teas and coffees. There are also curiosities such as salt diamonds from the Himalayas

Le Panier Gourmand, *1 rue du Plô, T04 68 25 15 63. Open 1030-2000.* Gourmet speciality shop in the Cité, selling goodies from across Languedoc.

Les Halles, *Rue de Verdun/rue Aimé-Ramond. Mon-Sat 0800-1300.* Historic U-shaped market near Place Carnot, which has recently been restored to its full glory.

Housewares

Esprit de Sel, *10 rue de la République, T04 68 72 03 01, www.espritdesel.fr. Tue-Sat 1000-1230 and 1430-1900.* A trove of traditional and designer furnishings and goods for the home and garden. Also sells soaps and beauty products.

Maison Coste, *40 rue Coste Rebouhl, T04 68 77 12 15, maison-coste.com. Mon-Fri 1400-1900, Sat 1000-1900.* A lovely boutique selling items for the home, including scented balls of *terre d'Anduze*.

What to do

Carcassonne and around *p21*
Boat trips

Lou Gabaret & Hélios, *27 rue des Trois Courronnes, T04 68 71 61 26, carcassonne-croisiere.com.* Ninety-minute trips on the Canal du Midi, departing from the car park near the train station.

Children

02 Aventure, *Lac de la Cavayère, 7 km southeast of Carcassonne, T04 68 25 33 83, wanside2.wordpress.com.* The Lac de la Cavayère is great for swimming but if you want more thrills, spend a couple of hours hanging from the trees and swinging like Tarzan from the branches.

Golf

Golf de Carcassonne, *Rte de St-Hilaire, T04 68 72 57 30, golf-de-carcassonne.com.* Handsome 18-hole par 71 course with views of the Black Mountains and Pyrenees.

Transport

Carcassonne and around *p21*
There are huge pay car parks outside the Porte Narbonne of the Cité, linked from in July and August by a free shuttle bus to the Cité. For a taxi, call T04 68 71 50 50.

The bus station is on Boulevard Varsovie; service to some towns is provided by **Kéolis**, 2 boulevard Paul Sabatier, T04 68 25 13 74, and **Tessier**, Le Pont Rouge, T04 68 25 85 45. The train station is at Port du Canal du Midi.

You can hire a bike at **Evasion2Roues**, 85 allée d'Iéna, T04 68 11 90 40, evasion2roues. eu. Tuesday-Thursday 0900-1200 and 1400-1900, Friday 0900-1900, Saturday 0900-1800.

Directory

Carcassonne and around *p21*
Money ATMs at **Banque Populaire**, Rue du Comte Roger up in the Cité; **Société Générale**, 6 place Carnot. **Medical services** Hospital: **Centre Hospitalier Antoine Gayraud**, Route de St-Hilaire, T04 68 24 24 24. Pharmacy: **Barbacane**, 110 rue Barbacane; Roux Barnet, 10 rue Courtejaire. **Post office** 40 rue Jean Bringer, T04 68 11 71 13. **Tourist information** 28 rue de Verdun, T04 68 10 24 30, carcassonne-tourisme.com. April-June, September-October Monday-Saturday 0900-1800, Sunday 0900-1300; July-August daily 0900-1900. November-March Monday-Saturday 0900-1230, 1330-1800. There's another office just inside the Porte Narbonnaise.

The Razès

This is one of the most interesting historical regions in the Aude, or at least the one that, since the 17th century, has been the most investigated, scrutinized and scoured for secrets and treasures. If nothing else, they've found a lot of dinosaur bones.

Rennes-le-Château and around

High on its hill, with commanding views over the Razès, tiny Rennes-le-Château has long been the vortex of Languedocien weirdness. Was Jesus really buried here after coming to France with his wife Mary Magdalene and raising a family? Did the Visigoths come here to hide the Ark of the Covenant? Did three Cathars escape from Monségur and bring a 'secret' here? Over 100,000 visitors come every year to see what it's all about.

Ste-Marie Magdalene

ⓘ *Rue de l'Eglise. Nov-Apr daily 1000-1300 and 1400-1715, Mid-May-Jun to Sep-Dec daily 1000-1815, Jul to mid-Sep daily 1000-1915.*

This church, which is on the same spot as a Visigothic chapel, was remodelled over seven years by the Abbé Saunière, the central figure in Rennes-le-Château's mysteries, and it is certainly odd. Terribilis est locus iste (this is a terrible place) reads the inscription over the door, and a leering demon supports the holy water stoup. The confessional is strangely located near the door – does it hide the secret entrance to the crypt? There are statues of Mary and Jesus, each holding a baby Jesus, fuelling speculation of possible twins. The Stations of the Cross run anti-clockwise.

The mystery of Rennes-le-Château

It all began in the 17th century, when a local shepherd found a cache of gold and then died without saying where. Suddenly, some very powerful people became interested in the Razès, among them Nicolas Poussin who painted the *Shepherds of Arcadia* with the inscription "Et in Arcadia ego" and Rennes in the background. The last lady of the Razès, the Dame de Blanchefort died in 1781. Her tombstone in Rennes-le-Château's cemetery read "Et in Arcadia ego".

The village declined until the 1890s, when its parish priest Bérenger Saunière received a 1000 franc donation to restore the church. Soon, he and his housekeeper Marie Dénarnaud were seen digging in the cemetery around the Dame de Blanchefort's tomb (which he defaced) and he asked the Louvre for a copy of Poussin's painting. He then began spending money – the equivalent of €2.5 million – building the Villa Bethania and the Tour Magdala, constructing a new road and bringing in running water.

Where did the money come from?

Many believe that during his restoration work on Ste-Marie Magdalene, Saunière discovered something in the altar – a clue, a treasure map or knowledge that enabled him to blackmail the Vatican. He was suspended from the priesthood when he refused to explain his wealth to the diocese. The priest who heard Saunière's deathbed confession in 1917 refused to administer the last rites. When Marie Dénarnaud sold the Villa Bethania in 1946, she promised to tell the new owner the secret before she died – only she had a fit and died speechless, in 1953.

A local newspaper wrote about Saunière in 1956, inspiring journalist Gérard de Sède's 1966 novel *L'Or de Rennes*. This in turn inspired Pierre Plantard and Phillippe de Chérisey to plant forged documents on a secret organization they called the 'Priory of Sion' in the Bibliothèque Nationale in Paris. Michael Baigent, Richard Leigh and Henry Lincoln's *Holy Blood Holy Grail* followed in 1982, beginning an esoteric industry popularized by *The Da Vinci Code*.

Domaine de l'Abbé Saunière: Boutique du Presbytère

ⓘ *Rue de l'Eglise, T04 68 31 38 85, rennes-le-chateau.fr.7 Jan-Feb Sat, Sun 1000-1300 and 1400-1715; Mar-Apr, Mid-Sep-Sep daily 1000-1815; May-Jun daily 1000-1815; Jul to mid-Sep daily 1000-1915; Oct-mid Dec daily 1000-1300 and 1400-1715, . €4.50, €3.50 concession.*

The village now owns Saunière's Villa Bethenia, which he never lived in. The visit takes in the much-studied pillar with the upside down cross of St Peter, believed to be Visigothic; the mysterious 'Dalle des Chevaliers', once part of the Carolingian altar chancel; the altar balustrade where Saunière may have found the clue that led him to his mysterious wealth; as well as the oratory, orangerie and picturesque Tour Magdala, Saunière's library and office.

Dinosauria

ⓘ *Espéraza, T04 68 74 26 88/T04 68 74 02 08, dinosauria.org. Jul-Aug daily 1000-1900, Feb-Jun, Sep-Nov half-term and Christmas school holidays daily 1030-1230 and 1330-1730. €8.70, €6.20 student/child (5-12), €25.80 family of 4, under 5s free. Visits to the digs Jul-Aug Mon-Sat €3.50, €2.50 child.*

This corner of Languedoc isn't only famous for mysteries. France's first dinosaur museum opened in 1992 in Espéraza, and was soon so full that an extension was added to house the fossils and reconstructed skeletons of 35 different dinosaurs found in nearby Campagne-sur-Aude. In July and August you can watch them bring new fossils to light, in the biggest palaeontology dig in Europe.

Musée de la Chapellerie

ⓘ *2 av de la Gare, Espéraza, T04 68 74 00 75,. Jan-Jun, Sep-Oct daily 1030-1230 and 1330-1730, Jul-Aug 1000-1900 daily, Nov-Dec 1400-1800. Free.*

Before dinosaurs, Espéraza was best known for its hats. Up until the early 1950s, 14 factories employed 3000 people, making the area the second-biggest maker of wool felt hats in the world. Today, only one factory survives and it's in nearby Couiza. Learn how hats are made here, from sheep to fedora; there's a hat boutique as well.

The Razès listings

For Sleeping and Eating price codes and other relevant information, see page 10.

🛏 Where to stay

The Razès *p30*

€€€ Château des Ducs de Joyeuse, *Allée du Château, Couiza, T04 68 74 23 50, chateau-des-ducs.com. Mar to mid-Nov.* Built in the 16th century by the Lieutenant Governor of Languedoc, this handsome castle with its fat round towers has 23 spacious rooms and 12 junior suites that combine Renaissance touches (dark wood furniture, four-poster beds and fabrics) with modern comforts and luxurious bathrooms. There's a pool, or you can swim in the nearby Aude. Price includes buffet breakfast.

€ La Maison de Chapelier, *7 rue Elie Sermet, Espéraza, T04 68 74 22 49, esperaza.net.* This big bourgeoise mansion, built in 1923 by a hat maker, has five big rooms full of character and high ceilings, with much of the original decoration intact. The house has three living rooms open to guests, and a shady park. There's even a pool and a sauna with a wooden deck for soaking up the sun. No credit cards.

Self-catering

Domaine de Mournac, *Antugnac, T04 68 74 21 10, mournac.com.* Located 8 km northwest of Rennes-le-Château, this beautiful stone-built property set in 9 ha dates back to the 11th century and was long used as a post house. It has three very stylish B&B rooms (€98-158), a studio and gîte sleeping 10 (from €900 a week). The views from the terrace and pool seem to go on forever.

Restaurants

The Razès *p30*

€€€ La Cour des Ducs, *Allée du Château, Couiza, T04 68 74 23 50, chateau-des-ducs.* *Mar to mid-Nov for dinner.* This elegant restaurant is the perfect setting for a feast; you can dine in the courtyard or in the stone-vaulted rooms of the Château des Ducs de Joyeuse. The food has a Provençal/Italian touch – mesclun salad, risotto, lamb cooked in the Niçoise style – and is accompanied by Corbières' finest wines.

€€€ Maison Gayda, *Brugairolles, T04 68 20 65 87, maisongayda.com. Wed-Sat for lunch and 1900-2100, Sun for lunch and 1800-2000.* This high-tech vineyard, 10 minutes from Limoux, has a cutting-edge restaurant on top of the winery, with views in all directions. The menu features the likes of seared king prawns, red pepper and fresh coriander with Espelette jam, or roast suckling pig. Alternatively, enjoy a luxury barbecue in one of six private *paillotes* in the pines. Lunch menus €24, others start at €38.

What to do

The Razès *p30*

Esoteric

Enigma Tours, *5 Grand' Rue, Rennes-le-Château, T04 68 74 34 47, enigmatours.net.* Spend a week trying to work out what's going on in Rennes-le-Château.

Rafting

Pyrenees Outdoor, *St-Martin-Lys (south of Quillan), T06 19 36 16 47, pyrenees-outdoor-sports.com.* Whitewater rafting, hydrospeed (body boarding) and canyoning down the Aude in the Gorge de St Georges and also in the Défilé de la Pierre-Lys. They also hire out mountain bikes.

Rodeo Raft, *3 quartier de la Condamine, Belvianes (south of Quillan), T04 68 20 98 86, rodeoraft.com.* Guided inflatable rafting trips, 'canoe hot-dog', hydrospeed and canyoning down the Aude.

Wellbeing

Rennes-les-Bains, *T04 68 74 71 00,.*

renneslesbains.com. Village spa offering jacuzzi, hamman, massages and an outdoor hot-water pool suitable for the whole family. €5.50, €2.50 child (3-12).

Wine classes

Vinécole, *Domaine de Gayda, Chemin de Moscou, Brugairolles, T04 68 31 64 14, vinecole.com*. Just north of Limoux, this wine school specializing in Languedoc-Roussillon offers 'intelligent' wine-tasting, classes and seminars in English.

Transport

The Razès *p30*

In July and August Rennes is closed to vehicles; leave your car in one of the car parks along the road up the hill; a little train functions as a free shuttle up to the town.

Corbières and Cathar castles

The Corbières is a stunning, if sparsely populated region striped with vines between wild rocks tufted with Mediterranean scrub and castles balanced on vertiginous ridges. The Gauls who refused to get along with the Romans were the first to hide here. It later became the front line between the Visigoths and the Saracens, but it was most famous during the Albigenisan Crusade, when its castles, built in the 10th and 11th centuries by the Counts of Besalú in Catalonia, provided last refuges for the Cathars.

These days, the Corbières is synonymous with wine. It's nothing new, as the soil here isn't good for much else, but since the 1980s the wine has improved in leaps and bounds, as switched-on vignerons have learned to maximize the mosaic of soils, exposures and microclimates. Much of the wine is produced in village cooperatives, and quite a few of these are open for visits; Bizanet and Douzens are the main centres.

Cathar castles

These count, if nothing else, as some of the most strikingly picturesque castles ever built. Their masters were Cathars, and after their demise, when the Treaty of Corbeil (1258) set the border between France and Aragon, the castles guarded the front lines as the 'five sons of Carcassonne'. Like Carcassonne, they lost their raison d'être when the Treaty of the Pyrenees moved the border to the Pyrenees, and fell into ruin. But what ruins.

Château de Termes and around

ⓘ Termes, T04 68 70 09 20, chateau-termes.com. Mar, Nov to mid-Dec Sat-Sun and school national holidays (or phone ahead) 1000-1700, Apr-Jun, Sep-Oct daily 1000-1800, Jul-Aug daily 1000-1930. €4, €2 child (6-15); €3 (student).

The Termenès is the wildest corner of the Corbières, and its castle stands in a strategic spot high over the River Sou. Its lord was the elderly Viscount Raymond, the brother of the Cathar parfait Benoît de Termes, who famously debated religion with St Dominic at the Colloquy of Montréal in 1207.

In 1210, after conquering Carcassonne, Minerve and Béziers, Simon de Montfort dragged his catapults here. The siege was a stalemate for three months, until the castle's water supply turned stagnant. Afflicted with dysentery, the defenders fled one night through a secret passage, but Viscount Raymond was hauled off to prison in Carcassonne where he died.

His son Olivier de Termes became one of France's greatest knights, and after trying to retake Carcassonne for the Trencavels, he submitted to the king and was chosen as a leader of the Seventh Crusade. In gratitude St Louis returned the Termenès to his family. He brought about the final peaceful surrender of Cathar Quéribus, accompanied Louis to Tunis on his ill-fated Eighth Crusade and died in Jerusalem in 1274.

Unlike the other Cathar castles, Termes was blown up by royal order in the 17th century, so only the outer walls and a few ruins remain, but the views into the ravines are spectacular.

For a more complete castle, head east to 13th-century **Villerouge-Termenès**, where the very last Cathar parfait Guilhem Bélibaste was burned at the stake in 1321. Learn more about him and life in the 14th century from the fascinating **audiovisual tour** ⓘ T04 68 70 09 11, Mar Sat-Sun 1000-1700, Apr-Jun, Sep to mid-Oct Mon-Fri 1000-1300 and 1400-1800, Sat-Sun 1000-1800, Jul-Aug daily 1000-1930, mid-Oct to mid-Dec Sat-Sun and national holidays 1000-1700 – 1 Nov 1000-1300 and 1400-1700 – €6, €2 young person/child 6-15, in English.

Château d'Aguilar

ⓘ Tuchan, T04 68 45 51 00. Apr to mid-Jun 1000-1800, mid-Jun to mid-Sep 0900-1900, mid-Sep-3 Nov 1100-1700. €3.50, €1.50 young person/child (10-15), under 10s free.

Although its name means 'eagle', the 13th-century castle of Aguilar, set on a relatively low outcrop amid a sea of vines, is the tamest looking of the Cathar castles. A possession of Termes, captured by Simon de Montfort in 1210, it was sold by Olivier de Termes to fund the Abbaye de Fontfroide. The French maintained a garrison here, although it was constantly threatened and finally abandoned in 1561 after Charles V captured it for Spain.

Château de Peyrepertuse

ⓘ Duilhac-sous-Peyrepertuse, T04 82 53 24 07, chateau-peyrepertuse.com. Feb daily 1000-

1700,Mar, Oct daily 1000-1800, Apr 0930-1900, May, Jun and Sep daily 0900-1900, Jul-Aug daily 0900-2000. €6 from Sep-Jun; €8.50 in Jul & Aug, €3 young person/child (6-15), audio guides €4. Visits are suspended during stormy weather. Check the website for special events.

Peyrepertuse ('pierced rock') is a breathtaking sight, teetering on a narrow 780-m precipice. Its walls encompass the same area as the Cité de Carcassonne but it's in such an impossible position that no one has ever attacked it.

The walls actually protect two castles. The lower one, begun in the ninth century by the Count of Besalú, belonged to Guillaume de Peyrepertuse. He gave it up in 1240, after the son of Roger Raymond Trencavel failed in his attempt to re-take Carcassonne. You can explore the triangular courtyard, the old keep, the curtain walls, the chapel of Ste Marie and the medieval latrines. The second, higher castle, was added by Louis XI and was built around the Donjon de St Jordi atop a steep stone stair.

Château de Quéribus and around

ⓘ *Cucugnan, T04 68 45 03 69, cucugnan.fr. Jan-Dec 1000-1700, Feb 1000-1730, Mar 1000-1800, Apr-Jun and Sep 0930-1900, Jul-Aug 0900-2000, Oct 1000-1830, €5.50, €3 young person/child (6-15).*

Some 9 km southeast of Peyrepertuse (and in easy signalling distance) the vertigo-defying Quéribus castle seems to grow organically from its pinnacle, with views from the top terrace (728 m) that stretch from the sea to the Pyrenees. Its lord, Pierre de Cucugnan, was a fierce protector of the Cathars and his castle turned out to be their very last bastion before they finally surrendered to Olivier de Termes in 1255, 11 years after Montségur. It's one of the most intact of the castles: the keep, defended by three outer walls, still has a flamboyant Gothic hall.

A long way below is **Cucugnan** and its windmill, a village famous in literature. Alphonse Daudet's tale, *Le Curé de Cucugnan* (in his *Lettres de Mon Moulin*) recounts a fire-eating sermon given by the village priest after he dreamed of a visit to Heaven and Hell in search of his parishioners. From May to October there's a free audiovisual *And if the story of Cucugnan was told to me* in the little Theatre Achille Mir (the name of the local author of the original tale in Occitan), which is on Place du Plantane (T04 68 45 09 09). The village **church** houses a rare statue of the Pregnant Virgin, who also bizarrely holds the baby Jesus in her arms.

Just west of Quéribus and Peyrepertuse, and north of St-Paul de Fenouillet, you can drive along the narrow windy road under the sheer cliffs and overhanging rock of the **Gorge de Galamus**, and perhaps spot its rare Bonelli eagles.

Château de Puilaurens

ⓘ *Puilaurens, T04 68 20 65 26. Feb, Mar Sat, Sun and school holidays 1000-1700; Apr, Oct to mid-Nov daily 1000-1700, May daily 1000-1800, Jun and Sep daily 1000-1900, Jul-Aug daily 0900-2000. €4, €2 young person/child (6-15).*

Built on a 700-m rocky outcrop, this castle was a 10th-century outpost of St Michel de Cuxa before it came under the Counts of Besalú and the kings of Aragon. Guillaume de Peyrepertuse arrived here after surrendering his own castle, followed by other *parfaits*, including some from Monségur, came here and defended Puilaurens under the last great Cathar military commander, Chabert de Barbaira. No one is quite sure what happened but by around 1250 history says that Puilaurens was under royal control as the southernmost citadel of France; Louis IX strengthened and garrisoned it with the largest number of troops. Spain attacked it on numerous occasions and captured it in 1635, shortly before having to give it back after the Treaty of the Pyrenees.

Much of what survives was built after 1250: the two curtain walls and four round towers defended the keep. The southwestern Tour de Dame Blanche recalls Blanche of Bourbon, who spent time at Puilaurens before she was murdered by her husband Pedro the Cruel of Castile; her ghost is said to be seen occasionally strolling across the wall. The tower has a rare relic, a built-in 'speaking tube' allowing communication between floors.

Corbières and Cathar castles listings

For Sleeping and Eating price codes and other relevant information, see page 10.

⊝ Where to stay

Corbières and Cathar castles *p35*
€€ Auberge de Cucugnan, *2 pl de la Fontaine, T04 68 45 40 84, auberge-de-cucugnan.com.* This comfortable family hotel, close to both Peyrepertuese and Quéribus, has small but tidy rooms and a warm welcome, and a superb restaurant, too: try the guinea fowl with cèpes cooked in Maury wine.
€ Ecluse du Soleil, *Sougraigne, T04 68 69 88 44, ecluseausoleil.com.* Peace and quiet is guaranteed in this hilltop hamlet 11 km south of Rennes-le-Château, with big views over the Pyrenees and en suite rooms spread among several stone houses. The owners know all about local activities, and there's tennis, a pool and restaurant serving tasty cuisine de terroir.

Restaurants

Corbières and Cathar castles *p35*
€€€€ Gilles Goujon, *5 av de St-Victor, Fontjoncouse, T04 68 44 07 37, aubergeduvieuxpuits.fr. Mar-May, Oct-Dec Wed-Sat for lunch and dinner, Sun for lunch; Jun-Sep Mon for dinner, Tue-Sun for lunch and dinner.* With three Michelin stars as of 2010, Gilles Goujon draws gourmets to tiny Fontjoncouse (pop. 100) east of Termes. His complex, creative, highly personal cuisine is constantly evolving, using only seasonal ingredients – in winter, for instance, wild hare (each cut of meat undergoes its own cooking method and is served with cocoa spaghetti and caramelized beetroot). Weekday lunch menu is €70. After your meal, you can choose to stay in Goujon's **Auberge du Vieux Puits** (aubergeduvieuxpuits.fr) around a Hollywood-style pool.
€€ Auberge du Vigneron, *2 rue Achille-Mir, Cucugnan, T04 68 45 03 00, auberge-vigneron. com. Mid-Feb to Jun, Sep to mid-Nov Tue-Sat for lunch and dinner, Sun for lunch, Jul-Aug daily for lunch, Mon-Sat for dinner.* Exploring Cathar castles is hungry work and this restaurant in a former wine cellar has a good choice of food – duck stewed with olives and mushrooms, bream and onion tarte, langoustines with asparagus. They also have a handful of rooms (€€). Menus start at €22.

Narbonne and around

Founded in 118 BC, Narbo Martius was Rome's first successful colony and the ancient capital of Languedoc, then known as Gallia Narbonensis. Yet, only bits from Roman times have survived. Instead, its startling centrepiece was left by its 12th- to 14th-century viscounts, who gave it a stupendous if abbreviated Gothic cathedral and archbishop's palace. Narbonne is a likeable little city, and when you need a break from all the history, the leafy quays of Canal de la Robine are never far.

Narbonne

Cathédrale St-Just-et-St Pasteur
① Rue Armand Gautier, T04 68 32 09 52. Oct-Jun daily 1000-1200 and 1400-1800, Jul-Sep daily 1000-1900. Trésor de la Cathédrale Nov-mid Jul Wed-Sat 1400-1745, Jul-Oct Mon-Sat 1000-1200, 1400-1745. €2.20.

Begun in 1272 by Pope Clement IV, a former archbishop of Narbonne, this Cathedral was designed to rival the soaring Gothic masterpieces of the Ile de France. It would have succeeded, too, had the city fathers not got with cold feet in 1340 when it came to demolishing part of the town wall. So the cathedral project came to an abrupt end, leaving a splendid choir and transept – and a blank wall where the nave should have been. From the Cour St-Eutrope, you can see signs of the architects' unfulfilled ambition – the walls, truncated pillars and flying buttresses.

Inside, the church's stumpiness makes the 130-ft **choir** seem even higher than it is. There's an enormous organ in a madly ornate wooden case that took a century to complete, beautiful stained glass from the 13th and 14th centuries, sumptuous tombs of archbishops and knights and a 14th-century polychrome stone *Déposition*. In 1981, the cathedral's 14th-century Gothic **retable**, broken and hidden during a remodelling in 1732, was rediscovered and has now been restored. It has some 200 figures, including vivid scenes of Purgatory, Hell and Limbo. The **treasury**, entered by way of the right ambulatory chapel, has a remarkable pair of 16th-century Flemish tapestries: one on the seven days of the *Creation*, the other an *Allegory on Prosperity and Adversity*. It is also home to beautiful gold and silver work, crystal cases, ivories and illuminated manuscripts.

The monumental but worn 14th- and 15th-century **cloisters** link the cathedral to the Palais des Archevêques by way of the **Passage de l'Ancre**.

Place de l'Hôtel-de-Ville and Palais des Archevêques
This big square is the busiest in Narbonne, and has been since the city's foundation. A slice of pavement has been cut away to reveal a section of **Via Domitia**. Looming over all is the **Palais des Archevêques**, an ecclesiastical fortress residence that in size and importance is surpassed in France only by the Papal Palace in Avignon. There are actually two palaces: the 'old' palace from the 12th century on the right, and the 'new' palace from the 14th century on the left, with a façade restored by Viollet-le-Duc. The complex is now home to Narbonne's Mairie (note the relief over the door, recalling the city's early maritime vocation) and its two most important museums.

Musée Archéologique
① Palais des Archevêques, Place de l'Hôtel-de-Ville, T04 68 90 30 54. Apr-mid Jul Wed-Mon 1000-1200 and 1400-1700; mid Jul-Oct daily 1000-1300 and 1430-1800; Nov-Mar Tue-Sun Wed-Mon 1400-1700. €4.

France's third most important archaeological collection outside Paris, Narbonne's museum has a rich pre-Roman collection of Bronze Age swords and Greek ceramics, as well as finds from the Gallo-Roman city. The museum's best-known treasures are the extremely rare, well-preserved frescoes that once adorned the homes of the smart set in the Clos de la Lombarde. Also look out for milestones from the Via Domitia, statues, sarcophagi and artefacts relating to daily life and the ancient port.

Musée d'Art et d'Histoire

ⓘ *Palais des Archevêques, Place de l'Hôtel-de-Ville, T04 68 90 30 54. Apr-mid Jul Wed-Mon 1000-1200 and 1400-1700; mid Jul-Oct daily 1000-1300 and 1430-1800; Nov-Mar Tue-Sun Wed-Mon 1400-1700. €4.*

This museum occupies the princely 17th- and 18th-century apartments of the archbishop of Narbonne, once the most powerful prelates in the South of France. The **Salle des Audiences** has a portrait of the last archbishop, Dillon, who also served as President of the Estates of Languedoc and did much to help Narbonne before the Revolution forced him into exile in London. In 2006 his tomb was exhumed at St Pancras during work on the Eurostar station, and in 2009 his remains were interred in Narbonne cathedral (except for his porcelain dentures, which are in the Museum of London).

Earlier archbishops not only lived like princes but hosted them: both Louis XIII and Louis XIV stayed in the **Chambre du Roi**, with a Roman mosaic floor and frescoed ceiling. In art, episcopal taste tended towards the Italians and the academic: in the **Grande Galérie** and **Oratoire** are paintings by Salvator Rosa, Canaletto, Rosalba Carriera, Ribera and other followers of Caravaggio, Breughel, and best of all, *Le Sacre de Roi David*, by Veronese. The **Salle des Faïences** houses 18th-century pharmacy jars and enamels from leading French centres (Moustiers, Sèvres, Montpellier). Lastly, the museum has a compelling **Orientalist Gallery**, housing a collection of 19th-century paintings on North African and Middle Eastern themes, some realistic, some imaginary, and displayed in rooms designed with motifs from the Great Mosque of Córdoba and a Moroccan Palace.

Donjon Gilles Aycelin

ⓘ *Place de l'Hôtel de Ville, access through the Mairie. Apr-mid Jul Wed-Mon 1000-1200 and 1400-1700; mid Jul-Oct daily 1000-1300 and 1430-1800; Nov-Mar Tue-Sun Wed-Mon 1400-1700. €4..*

The 13th-century Archbishop Gilles Aycelin built this 41-m tower just to show he was in charge; there are great views over the city from the top.

Horreum Romain

ⓘ *7 rue Rouget de Lisle. Apr-mid Jul Wed-Mon 1000-1200 and 1400-1700; mid Jul-Oct daily 1000-1300 and 1430-1800; Nov-Mar Tue-Sun Wed-Mon 1400-1700. €4.*

The ancient geographer Strabo called *Narbo Martius* the 'greatest emporium' in the south of France, and these long subterranean galleries (a *horreum* is a granary) from the first century BC are proof that he wasn't full of baloney. Hollowed out in the form of a giant 'U', arms, grain, oil and wine were stored here at a constant 12-14°C. Two of the wings are open, equipped with a sound and light evocation of Roman Narbo.

Canal de la Robine

In Roman times, before the river silted up and moved, ships could sail up the Aude to Narbonne. With the success of the Canal du Midi, Narbonne wanted a piece of the action, and in 1686 the Aude's ancient bed was made into the Canal de la Robine, reattaching the city to its long-lost river. From there, goods were transported overland to Le Somail until 1776, when the Canal de Jonction provided a direct link to the Canal du Midi.

Today, the Canal de la Robine doubles as Narbonne's favourite promenade. The southern stretch is dominated by the beautiful **Halles** built in 1905, not far from the **Pont des Marchands**, Nabonne's 'Little Ponte Vecchio' – the only bridge in France with buildings. Underneath are the arches of the Roman bridge that carried the Via Domitia over the Aude.

Basilique St Paul-Serge and around

ⓘ *Rue de l'Hôtel Dieu, T04 68 90 30 65. Mon-Sat 0900-1200 and 1400-1800.*

This handsome church of 1180, the third on this site, was one of the first in the south to be built in the new Gothic style. It stands over the tomb of St Paulus-Sergius, the first bishop of Narbonne. The interior, with its massive choir, vaults and arcades, is stunning; the holy water stoup has a little frog, which according to legend was petrified by an archbishop when it started to croak heresy during Mass. Ask to visit the **Paleochristian crypt** (AD 250), containing the oldest Christian sarcophagi in Gaul, in what was originally a shared pagan/ Christian necropolis along the road to Bordeaux.

The adjacent hospital is built around the medieval incarnation, or **Hôtel Dieu**, which incorporates a fancy baroque chapel from 1782. Further along rue de l'Hôtel Dieu stands one of the finest Renaissance houses in Languedoc, known as the **Maison des Trois-Nourrices** (1558) (House of the Three Wet Nurses) after the busty caryatids around the windows.

Maison Natale de Charles Trénet

ⓘ *13 av Charles-Trénet, T04 68 90 30 66. Apr-mid Jul Wed-Mon 1000-1200 and 1400-1700; mid Jul-Oct daily 1000-1300 and 1430-1800; Nov-Mar Tue-Sun Wed-Mon 1400-1700. €6.*

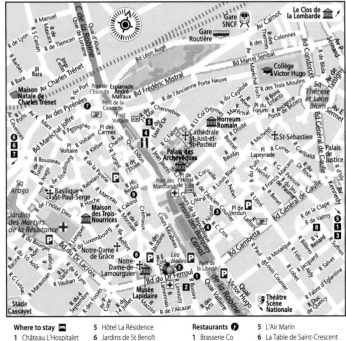

Where to stay		Restaurants	
1 Château L'Hospitalet	5 Hôtel La Résidence	1 Brasserie Co	5 L'Air Marin
2 Hôtel de France	6 Jardins de St Benôît	2 Chez Bébelle	6 La Table de Saint-Crescent
3 Hôtel de la Clape	7 La Demeure de	3 Cocodélices	7 Le Petit Comptoir
4 Hôtel de Paris	Roquelongue	4 En Face	8 Les Cuisiniers Cavistes
	8 Le Régent		9 Les Ramplas

Singer and songwriter, Charles Trénet (1913-2001), nicknamed *le fou chantant* (the singing fool), donated his birthplace near the train station to the city on the condition that it didn't become a museum. Instead it has remained as it was, with its piano, old photos and furnishings. The sound system plays Trénet's biggest hits, including *Y a d'la joie!*, surely the happiest song ever recorded.

Notre-Dame-de-Lamourguier and Musée Lapidaire

ⓘ *Place Emile Digeon. Apr-mid Jul Wed-Mon 1000-1200 and 1400-1700; mid Jul-Oct daily 1000-1300 and 1430-1800; Nov-Mar Tue-Sun Wed-Mon 1400-1700. €4.*

With nearly 2000 inscriptions, tombs, altars, stelae and sculptures, this 13th-century Benedictine church holds the second largest lapidary museum anywhere outside Rome. Most were incorporated into the city walls, and recovered when the walls were dismantled. Audiovisual images of ancient and medieval buildings put them in context.

Le Clos de la Lombarde

ⓘ *Rue de Chanzy, T04 68 90 30 54. Sep-Jun guided tours by appointment, Jul-Aug daily 1000-1200 and 1500-1900, €6.*

This cluster of six Roman houses along the Via Domitia has been the focus of archaeological excavations since 1974. The paintings it has yielded are on display in the Archaeology Museum.

Around Narbonne

Abbaye de Fontfroide

ⓘ *D 613, 12 km southwest of Narbonne, T04 68 45 11 08, fontfroide.com. Guided 60-75 minute tours at 1000, 1100, 1200, 1400, 1500 and 1600. Tours in French, English audio guide provided. €9.50; €6 young person (16-25), €3.50 child (6-15). Gardens open May-Sept €6, €3.50 ages 6-15; Musée Fayet -Sept €6, €3.50 ages 6-15. Combine two sites for €12.50, €10.50 ages 16-25, €6 ages 6-15; all three for €18.50, €16 ages 16-25, €6 ages 6-15.*

Isolated amid the wooded hills, Fontfroide was the most powerful Cistercian monastery in the south. It was founded by the Viscount of Narbonne in 1093 and adopted Cistercian rule after being visited by St Bernard in 1145. It rapidly grew in importance, with fingers in many political pies and monks and abbots who acted on an international stage: Pierre de Castelnau, the Papal Legate who was assassinated in Beaucaire, triggering the Albigensian Crusade in 1209; another abbot was Papal Legate in the trial against the Templars; and Jacques Fournier was elected pope Benedict XII in Avignon in 1317. At the abbey's peak, its surrounding farms and vines supported a community of 300. In 1348, the Black Death killed all but 20 monks.

Fontfroide recovered, but like many Cistercian houses it gradually became more worldly. In 1791 the last monks left, and the abbey managed the rare feat of escaping the Revolution undamaged. It even knew a brief revival from 1858-1908 when it was home to a community from Sénaque.

The tour takes in courtyards worthy of palaces, the large vaulted refectory and the elegant late 12th-century cloister, with its lace work of arches set in arches. The majestic church, towering 20 m at the crossing, was begun right after St Bernard's visit, and has colourful stained-glass windows added in the 1920s. Collages of older stained glass collected from churches in northern France after the First World War decorate the dormitories.

The abbey's rose garden, in the former cemetery of the monks, has some 3000 bushes, including many medieval varieties, and at least as many butterflies. Another ticket gives access to the main gardens, where the 16th century terraces have been replanted. In 2008, the Musée Gustav Fayet was set up in a part of the abbey formerly closed to visitors to display the works of the artist who purchased Fontfroide in 1908 and began its restoration.

Narbonne's coast

A big chunk of *garrigue*, the vine-covered **Montagne de La Clape**, separates Narbonne from the Aude's seaside playground.

St-Pierre-la-Mer and Narbonne Plage
Northernmost St-Pierre-la Mer has merged with Narbonne Plage, forming your basic beach resort. It does have something unique, however: there's an 800-m hike from the car park at St-Pierre, and hidden in the rocks is the turquoise freshwater pool known as **Gouffre de L'Oeil Doux**, under a sheer white cliff.

Gruissan Plage
Surrounded by flamingo-filled lagoons, Gruissan Plage has more character than those mentioned above. It has an old town that sweeps around a ruined tower, the **Tour de Barbarousse**. The tower was probably named after the Turkish pirate admiral, who in the 1540s was an ally of the French against Charles V. Gruissan is famous for its **Plage des Pilotis** – a wide beach backed by 1300 wooden cottages on stilts. The first were built in the 1850s when the craze for sea bathing took hold, back when the land flooded every winter. Many owners have since 'improved' them by cladding them in aluminium siding.

Sigean

The Réserve Africaine de Sigean
ⓘ *D 6009, Sigean, T04 68 48 20 20, reserveafricainesigean.fr. Nov-Feb 0900-1600 (last admission); Mar and Oct 0900-1700 (last admission); Apr-Sep 0900-1830 (last admission), other months vary by 30 mins. €28, €21 child (4-14).*

In a sunny landscape of *garrigue* and lagoons, the Sigean reserve opened in 1974 and has grown into one of the most popular attractions in Languedoc. No longer strictly reserved for African animals, it currently hosts 3800 mammals, lizards and birds, many of them rare and endangered (white rhinoceros, Somali ass, Tibetan bears). They roam freely over 300 ha, in various parks. Allow at the very least three hours by car and foot.

For Sleeping and Eating price codes and other relevant information, see page 10.

◉ Where to stay

Narbonne *p40, map p43*

€€€ Château L'Hospitalet, *Hospitalet, rte de Narbonne-Plage (D168), T04 68 45 28 50, chateau-lhospitalet.com*. Ten minutes south of Narbonne in the hills of La Clape, this recently refurbished wine château has 38 immaculate if slightly sterile rooms, each named after one of the wines. It's very peaceful, and there's a pool (or the beach, five minutes away) and a good restaurant called H. Guests are welcomed with a free bottle of wine.

€€€ La Demeure de Roquelongue, *53 av de Narbonne, St-André-de-Roquelongue, T04 68 45 63 57/T06 98 87 11 44, demeure-de-roquelongue.com*. This very stylish five-room B&B in a 19th-century townhouse has featured in a number of French design magazines. Located 12 km from Narbonne by the Abbaye de Fontfroide, it's also close to the Canal du Midi and Corbières. Each room is named after a wind: Espan has a wonderful old-fashioned bathtub in an alcove resembling a mini-theatre; the Eole rooms sleeps four. There's a large garden and the price includes an excellent breakfast.

€€ Hôtel de la Clape, *4 rue des Fleurs, Narbonne Plage, T04 68 49 80 15, hoteldelaclape.com*. This Logis de France, in a quiet area only 80 m from the beach, is equipped with a pool and makes an excellent choice for families, with rooms sleeping up to five. Rooms have air conditioning and many have balconies. The very welcoming hosts Corinne and Nicolas also have an excellent restaurant, with occasional jazz nights in summer.

€€ Hôtel La Résidence, *6 rue 1er Mai, T04 68 32 19 41, hotelresidence.fr*. This is a charming reworking of an old 19th-century hotel and is situated in the heart of Narbonne. It offers 26 classic rooms in soft pastels, most with unusually large bathrooms. There's a private garage, an internet area and they offer light meals, as well as wine tastings.

€ Hôtel de France, *6 rue Rossini, T04 68 32 09 75, hotelnarbonne.com*. This charming 15-room hotel on a quiet street has air conditioning, Wi-Fi, firm mattresses, satellite TV and parking. The owner speaks English. Closed February.

€ Hôtel de Paris, *2 rue du Lion d'Or, T04 68 32 08 68, hoteldeparis-narbonne.com*. This old budget standby offers basic but adequate rooms. Parking nearby is fairly easy (it's a 10-minute walk from the station), and room prices vary by the amount of plumbing you choose – the cheapest have bathrooms in the hall. Nevertheless, all rooms are equipped with Wi-Fi.

€ Le Régent, *15 rue Suffren and 50 rue Mosaïque, T04 68 32 02 41, leregent-narbonne. com*. Just south of the Boulevard Gambetta, this little 15-room hotel has recently been refurbished. All rooms are different, some have bathrooms and some have toilets down the hall, and some sleep five people. There are fine views over Narbonne from the roof terrace. There's a little garden; garden rooms Nos 16 and 17 are the nicest. Parking is easy, and they hoffer Wi-Fi and a garage for bikes.

Self-catering

Jardins de St Benoît, *Rte de Talairan, St-Laurent-de-la-Cabrerisse, T04 67 11 87 15, garrigae-resorts.com/Jardins-de-Saint-Benoit*. Inland from Sigean, this riverside spa-resort consists of 171 traditional one- to five-bedroom village-style houses, each with a garden and terrace (larger ones have private pools). Adjacent is the 'real' village of St-Laurent, which has a restaurant, spa, babysitters, children's club and designated gardens for picking vegetables. Off-peak special weekend offers start at €190 for a family of four.

Restaurants

Narbonne *p40, map p43*

€€€ L'Air Marin, *Bd Méditerranée, Narbonne Plage, T04 68 43 84 89, restaurantairmarin. com.* This waterfront restaurant draws seafood lovers year round with its delicious and fresh cuisine. There are mussels prepared in 10 different ways, oysters, *bourride narbonnais, sarsuela* (Catalan-style seafood 'opera'), lobster, gambas and much more, including salads and meat courses. The weekday lunch menu is €16.

€€€ La Table de Saint-Crescent, *68 av du Général Leclerc, T04 68 41 37 37, la-table-saint-crescent.com. Tue-Fri for lunch and dinner, Tue-Sat for dinner, Sun for lunch.* Elegant dining in a former oratory. Lionel Giraud's cuisine is inventive, and includes such dishes as salmon *tartare* with grilled sesame and sea lettuce, red peppers in clam juice and preserved lemon emulsion, or the surreally named *Conception d'une volaille sphérique* in morel cream, with asparagus, soy risotto and the quintessence of parmesan in spaghetti. Desserts and wines are equally astonishing. The three-course weekday €25 lunch menu is excellent value.

€€ Brasserie Co, *1 bd du Docteur Ferroul, T04 68 32 55 25. Mon-Sun 12-1430, Mon-Sat 1900-2200 .* This chic art-deco brasserie run by a charming *patronne* is near the market, and is where locals meet for a meal or just a coffee on the pavement terrace. The dishes are a real cut above typical brasserie fare, with the likes of *foie gras en millefeuille au caramel de figues.* The lunch *formule* is only €13.50; dinner menus start at €20.50.

€€ Le Petit Comptoir, *4 bd Maréchal Joffre, T04 68 42 30 35, petitcomptoir.com. Tue-Sat for lunch and dinner.* This resolutely retro restaurant – all dark wood and white linen – is one of the trendiest in Narbonne. The menu changes every week, but oysters and foie gras in various forms (and together) usually feature, along with classics such as fillet of beef en croûte and monkfish 'stitched' with anchovies, Gruissan style. Dinner menus start at €27.

€€ Les Cuisiniers Cavistes, *1 place Lamourguier, T04 682 96 45, cuisiniers-cavistes.com. Tue-Sat for lunch and dinner. The shop is open Tue-Sat 0900-1900.* This is an unusual restaurant/wine bar/shop highlighting 52 of the finest wines of Languedoc, which you can buy or drink on the spot accompanied by a gourmet lunch. They also sell specialities such as truffles, sun-dried tomatoes and bread baked in a 100-year-old wood-fired oven.

€ Chez Bébelle, *1 bd du Docteur Ferroul, T06 85 40 09 01, bar-chez-bebelle.com. Open 0600-1400.* Located in Narbonne's beautiful market, Les Halles, this is a great place for your morning meat fix: Bébelle was a rugby player and he makes great steaks.

€ En Face, *27 Cours de la République, T04 68 75 16 17. Thu-Mon for lunch and dinner, Tue for lunch.* This has a family atmosphere, red checked tablecloths and serves regional favourites such as cassoulet and *bourride.* It's such a favourite for lunch that it's best to arrive at exactly noon.

Cafés and bars

Cocodélices, *30 rue de l'Ancien-Courrier, T04 68 65 00 89. May-Sep Tue-Sun 0900-1900, Oct-Apr Tue-Sat 0900-1900.* Tea room/café serving delicious coffees, cappuccinos, teas and excellent cakes with home-made whipped cream.

Les Ramblas, *Place des Quatres-Fontaines, T04 68 49 68 11. Mon-Wed 0700-2200, Thu-Sat 0700-0200, Sun 1800-0200.* Trendy bar for those in their 20s, especially popular after dark when everyone meets before going clubbing.

Entertainment

Narbonne *p40, map p43*
Clubs
Chakana Club, *ZI Croix Sud, 300 m from the Narbonne Sud autoroute exit, facebook.com/chakanaclub. Thu-Sun.* This huge Ibiza-style

club attracts famous international DJs. It plays 1980s disco on the patio (heated and sheltered in winter) and House inside. Check their Facebook page for theme nights.

Dancing GM Palace, *Centre Commercial Forum Sud, rte de Perpignan, T04 68 41 59 71. Fri-Sat 2200-0500, Sun 1500-2000.* A retro disco that appeals to an older crowd, complete with a traditional Sunday 'tea dance'.

Le Théâtre Scène Nationale, *2 av Maître Hubert Mouly, T04 68 90 90 20, letheatre-narbonne.com.* New theatre with two auditoriums; one for plays, concerts and ballets and the other showing art movies.

Shopping

Narbonne *p40, map p43*
Food and drink
La Ferme Narbonnaise, *21-23 rue Droite, T04 68 49 57 01, la-ferme-narbonnaise.com. Mon 1100-1300 and 1430-1900, Tue-Sat 0900-1300 and 1430-1900.* Gourmet delicacies ranging from farm cheeses to olive oils, caviars, *rillettes de sardines* and champagne.
Les Halles, *1 bd du Docteur Ferroul. Open 0600-1400.* Narbonne's beautiful market built in 1905 has 70 stands offering the finest regional produce. On Thursdays and Sundays, stalls extend outside along the canal, selling clothes, flowers, etc.
Tendance & Gourmandise, *2 rue Raspail, Cours Mirabeau, T04 68 91 43 92, tendance-gourmandise.com, Tue-Sat 1000-1900.* Personalized sugar-coated almonds and chocolates and 23 flavours of macaroons, plus teas, coffees, foie gras and other goodies.

What to do

Narbonne *p40, map p43*
Birdwatching
Station orinthologique de Gruissan, *Rte de Tournebelle, T04 68 49 12 12.* Some 200 migratory species have been sighted here; in summer, spring and autumn naturalists offer free birdwatching walks (ring ahead for times).

Boat trips
Les Coches d'Eau du Patrimoine, *Cours Mirabeau, T04 689 12 40, cpie-narbonnais. org. Jul to mid-Sep.* See Narbonne from canal level or sail down to the Mediterranean on the Canal de la Robine to the nature reserve of Ile Ste-Lucie.
Promenades en Bateau L'Embarcadere, *32 cours de la République, T064 76 02 93. May to mid-Sep 1100-1900.* Hire a little electric boat for an hour or two on the Canal de la Robine.

Children
Espace de Liberté, *Rte de Perpignan, T04 68 42 17 89, espaceliberte.com.* Good for rainy days: a family-oriented leisure centre with pools, bowling alley and ice skating rink.

Walking
Le Sentier Cathar. Starting in Port-La-Nouvelle, this 12-stage 250-km path of the Cathars takes in the most beautiful scenery of the Corbières and Cathar sites and ends in Foix in the Pyrenees, passing through Montségur. Carcassonne-based **Areobus Haute-Vallée** (T04 68 20 15 54 or T06 68 72 05 01 (mobile), aerobus-hautevallee.com) can provide baggage forwarding. Organize room and board with UK-based **World Walks** (T+44 (0)1242-254353, worldwalks. com) or the Paris-based **Sentiers de France** (T02 47 41 67 07, sentiersdefrance.com).

Transport

Narbonne *p40, map p43*
It's usually easy to find street parking just outside the compact historic centre. Otherwise, park at the Parking Relais du Parc des Sports (follow the Canal de la Robine to avenue de la Mer) and catch the Line A shuttle into the centre. City bus No 8 goes to Gruissan Plage-Narbonne Plage-St-Pierre-la Mer; for schedules, T04 68 90 18. In July and

August, links to the beaches are increased and cost only €1.

The bus station is on Avenue Carnot, next door to the train station. The train station is on Avenue Carnot.

Directory

Narbonne *p40, map p43*

Money ATMs at **BNP-Paribas**, 50 rue Jean Jaurès; **Société Générale**, 3 cours République. **Medical services** Hospital: **Centre Hospitalier de Narbonne**, boulevard du Docteur Lacroix, T04 68 42 60 00. Pharmacy: **Des Halles**, 13 boulevard du Docteur Ferroul, T04 68 32 01 67; Pont des Marchands, 7 rue Pont des Marchands, T04 68 32 00 75. **Post office** 19 boulevard Gambetta, T04 68 65 88 64. **Tourist information** 31 rue Jean Jaurès, T04 68 65 15 60, narbonne-tourisme.com (mid-Sep to Mar Mon-Sat 1000-1230 and 1330-1800, Sun and national holidays 0900-1300; Apr to mid-Sep daily 0900-1900). From July to mid-September, the tourist office organizes a variety of guided tours (2500 years of history, Roman Narbonne, Medieval Narbonne etc); for more info, ring T04 68 90 30 66.. Tip: save money with a **Pass Monuments et Musées**. For €9 (€6 concessions) you can see the Horreum, Archaeology, Art and History and Lapidary museums; Donjon, Cathedral Treasure and Charles Trénet's birthplace. It's valid for 15 days.

Contents

Hérault

You could spend your whole holiday in the Hérault and never be bored. Montpellier, Languedoc-Roussillon's edgy, adrenalin-charged capital is urbane and sleek, enlivened by a huge student population, while its 17th-century predecessor Pézenas, the golden-stoned 'Versailles of Languedoc', daydreams of Molière. For seaside frolics you can choose between the futuristic resort of La Grande-Motte or fashionable Cap d'Agde, home to the excellent Musée de l'Ephèbe, which houses the region's finest antiquities. For salty character and delectable crustaceans, there's Sète and the fishing villages around the vast oyster nursery that is the Bassin de Thau.

Picturesque Béziers is the Hérault's second city, and nearby is the ancient oppidum of Ensérune, one of the best-preserved pre-Roman sites in France. Many of the *département's* finest vineyards are not far away in the Minervois, set between the languid meanders of the Canal du Midi – a magical 17th-century marvel of engineering. The sparsely populated mountains and *garrigue* in the northern Hérault have their splendours too – wild gorges, caves and rivers – and it's ideal country for trekking and canoeing. It's also worth exploring the cache of exceptional medieval villages here, headlined by St-Guilhem-le-Désert, Roquebrun, Minerve and Olargues.

Montpellier and around

Languedoc's capital, Montpellier (population: 240,000) is currently France's eighth largest city and growing like a weed, with 1000 new residents arriving every week. This is astounding considering it was number 25 back in 1977, when its controversial, go-getting mayor Georges Frêche was elected (he left in 2004, only to become president of the Languedoc-Roussillon region). Home to a major university, research institutes and 70,000 students, its historic core, L'Ecusson, offers a buzzing urbane cocktail of elegant *hôtels particuliers*, boutiques and restaurants. Although it's one of the very few French cities without ancient roots, Montpellier (founded in 985) has made up for this lack with an array of 'new' classics – Antigone, the Corum, the Odysseum and Mare Nostrum aquarium, the results of a building spree few can match.

Place de la Comédie and around

The Place de la Comédie, poised between the historic centre and the 'new' Montpellier, is the vortex where everyone and everything converges. With the **Fountain of the Three Graces** (1796) splashing in the centre, this is a square that would look at home in Paris, embraced as it is by the elegant 19th-century **Opéra Comédie** and Second Empire buildings sporting Mansard roofs, froufrou balconies and grand cafés. Cars were banned in 1985, but sleek trams glide along the edge.

The square extends north into the leafy **Esplanade Charles de Gaulle** and the **Jardin du Champ du Mars**, a popular city park with duck ponds and arty playgrounds anchored by one of Georges Frêche's pricey grands projets: the pink marble Corum (1988) housing a conference centre and the **Opéra Berlioz**.

Musée Fabre

ⓘ *39 bd de Bonne Nouvelle, T04 67 14 83 00, museefabre-en.montpellier-agglo.com. Tue, Thu, Fri and Sun 1000-1800, Wed 1300-2100, Sat 1100-1800. €6, €4 young person/child (6-18), family ticket €12. Hôtel Sabatier €4 (€2.50 young person/child (6-18); combined ticket €8, €6 young person/child (6-18), family ticket €15. Free on 1st Sun of every month.*

One of France's top provincial collections, the Fabre was founded in 1825 and re-opened in 2007 after a superb four-year restoration. There are some fine Dutch and Flemish Grand Masters, Veronese's richly coloured *Mystic Marriage of St Catherine*, Zurbarán's *St Agatha* and several works by Nicolas Poussin, including a poetic *Venus and Adonis* (1624) – or half of it. Recently, the rest of the painting was discovered in a private American collection and the museum is currently raising funds to buy it.

The Fabre is best known, however, for its 19th-century French art, donated by local benefactor Alfred Bruyas, who had his portrait painted by Delacroix, Courbet and every other artist he ever met. He also co-stars in the museum's best-known work: Gustav Courbet's jaunty *The Meeting*, celebrating the artist's arrival in Montpellier, but better known as *Bonjour, Monsieur Courbet* for the artist's prominent self portrait. Another featured canvas by Courbet, *Les Baigneuses*, caused such a scandal at the Paris Art Salon of 1853 that Napoleon III ordered it removed. Bruyas, who knew more about painting than the emperor, bought it. Soon artists were making pilgrimages to Montpellier to study what is now recognized as a pivotal work in the history of art.

Other highlights of the museum include luminous paintings by Montpelliérain Frédéric Bazille (a proto-Impressionist who died young) and works by Géricault, Ingres, Fragonard, David, Morisot, Sisley and Matisse. A new wing holds 20 paintings by contemporary artist Pierre Soulages, while just around the corner at 6 bis rue Montpellieret, the **Hôtel de Cabrières-Sabatier d'Espeyran** opened in 2010 with a collection of furniture and decorative arts.

Around l'Ecusson

Old Montpellier, named after its escutcheon shape on the map, is a fascinating tangle of streets, bijou squares, lovingly preserved *hôtels particuliers*, boutiques and little restaurants. From Place de la Comédie, head up **Rue de la Loge**, the city's high street, and midway you'll see a statue of assassinated Socialist Prime Minister Jean Jaurès standing like a benevolent guardian over the bustling pavement cafés in **Place Jean-Jaurès**. This

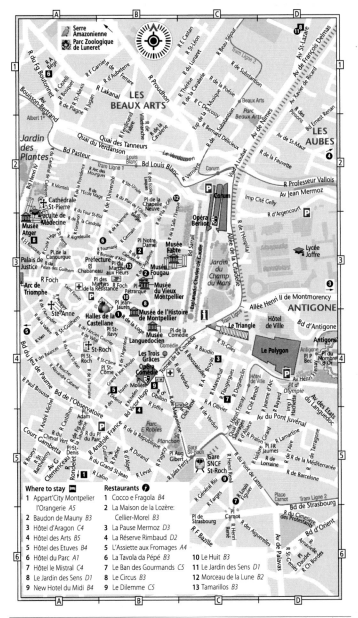

Serre
Amazonienne
Parc Zoologique
de Luneret

LES
BEAUX ARTS

LES
AUBES

Jardin
des
Plantes

Cathédrale
St-Pierre
Faculté de
Médecine
Musée
Atger

Palais de
Justice
Arc de
Triomphe

Préfecture

Pl Notre
Dame
Musée
Fabre

Marché
aux Fleurs

Musée
Fougau

Musée
du Vieux
Montpellier

Ste-Anne
Pl Jean-
jaurès

Musée de l'Histoire
de Montpellier

Halles de
la Castellane

Musée
Languedocien

St-Roch

Les Trois
Grâces
Opéra
Comédie

Corum

Opéra
Berlioz

Jardin
du
Champ
du Mars

ANTIGONE

Le Triangle

Hôtel
de Ville

Bd d'Antigone

Antigone

Le Polygon

Lycée
Joffre

Allée Henri II de Montmorency

Gare
SNCF
St-Roch

Place
Carnot

Where to stay 🛏
1 Appart'City Montpellier
  l'Orangerie *A5*
2 Baudon de Mauny *B3*
3 Hôtel d'Aragon *C4*
4 Hôtel des Arts *B5*
5 Hôtel des Etuves *B4*
6 Hôtel du Parc *A1*
7 Hôtel le Mistral *C4*
8 Le Jardin des Sens *D1*
9 New Hotel du Midi *B4*

Restaurants 🍴
1 Cocco e Fragola *B4*
2 La Maison de la Lozère:
  Cellier-Morel *B3*
3 La Pause Mermoz *D3*
4 La Réserve Rimbaud *D2*
5 L'Assiette aux Fromages *A4*
6 La Tavola du Pépé *B3*
7 Le Ban des Gourmands *C5*
8 Le Circus *B3*
9 Le Dilemme *C5*
10 Le Huit *B3*
11 Le Jardin des Sens *D1*
12 Morceau de la Lune *B2*
13 Tamarillos *B3*

square was once the site of the city's most important church, Notre-Dame-des-Tables, the 'tables' belonging to the money changers who did business with pilgrims to Compostela. Although the church was destroyed in the 16th-century Wars of Religion, the crypt survives and you can take a bizarre 'virtual tour' of the church and city in the **Musée de l'Histoire de Montpellier** ① *Tue-Sat 1030-1200 and 1330-1800, €3.*(combined admission with the Musée de Vieux Montpellier)

At the top of Rue de la Loge, the covered market, or the **Halles de la Castellane** (1869) stand at an important crossroad. To the left, busy Rue St-Guilhem runs past some of Montpellier's most picturesque medieval lanes: one, Rue Ste-Anne, leads to the tall neo-Gothic **St-Anne**, a church now used for art exhibitions.

If you're in a hurry, however, turn right at the top of Rue de la Loge, towards the Préfecture flanked by pretty squares. You'll find **Place du Marché aux Fleurs** and lovely little **Place Chabaneau**, both filled with popular pavement cafés.

In 1878, a section of the medieval town west of here was razed for broad **Rue Foch** and a Greek temple of a Palais de Justice. Near this, Rue Astuc leads just north to one of the city's best-loved squares: the tree-lined 17th-century **Place de la Canourgue** with a unicorn fountain.

Arc de Triomphe and Place du Peyrou

If Montpellier's Place de la Comédie echoes Paris, Paris also echoes Montpellier. Rue Foch, like a mini Champs Elysées, is closed off by an Arc de Triomphe that pre-dates Paris's by a century. It was erected to replace a medieval gate and to celebrate the triumphs of Louis XIV over heresy, England and the Holy Roman Empire, as well as the construction of the Canal du Midi.

Through the arc, at the city's highest point are the gardens of the Place du Peyrou, with their century-old magnolias and an equestrian statue of Louis XIV. The original was cast in Paris, but by the time it made it to Montpellier after the boat carrying it sunk in the Garonne, the Roi Soleil was dead. During the Revolution it was smashed to bits; the current copy dates from 1838. Behind it stands the hexagonal water tower or **Château d'Eau**, into which flowed the waters of the 18th-century **St-Clément aqueduct** that stretches majestically to the west on arches inspired by the Pont du Gard.

Cathédrale St-Pierre

① *Place Cathédrale St-Pierre. Daily 0900-1200, Mon-Sat 1430-1900.*
Tall, austere St-Pierre was the college of St-Benoît's church before it was converted into a cathedral in 1563, only to be wrecked during the Wars of Religion and the Revolution. The striking porch with its rocket-like towers is the only original feature to survive. Of the paintings inside, the best is Montpellier-native Sébastien Bourdin's *Fall of Simon Magus* (1657) in the right transept.

Faculté de Médecine

① *Rue de l'Ecole-de-Médecine. Open on guided tours only with the tourist office, T04 67 60 19 19 (the more who join, the cheaper it is).*
Montpellier has long had a medical vocation: its medical school was founded in 1220 by teachers who had learned their profession through the city's trading contacts with the Levant and the famous medical school in Salerno, Italy – making it the world's oldest, still functioning medical school. In 1289 Pope Nicolas issued a bull that put Montpellier's Studium Generalis – its university of medicine, law and the arts – on the same level as those of Paris and Bologna.

The current building began as the monastic college of St-Benoît, built in 1364 by Pope Urban V (a former teacher), who employed the same architects as had designed Avignon's Papal Palace: during the Revolution, it all became strictly secular. The most famous alumni were Rabelais and Nostradamus, neither of whom were known, however, for their doctoring. Visits run by the tourist office include the Amphithéâtre Saint-Côme and the Pharmacie de la miséricorde) and the building's portraits of 200 great doctors; another tour takes in the fascinating if rather stomach-churning Anatomy Museum (no pregnant women or under 12s allowed).

Musée Atger
① 2 rue de l'Ecole-de-Médecine, T04 34 43 35 81. Mon, Wed and Fri 1330-1745. Free.
Located within the Faculté de Médecine, this is the oldest museum in Montpellier, the home to a superb collection of French, Flemish and Italian drawings and prints (on sliding panels). All were donated by Xavier Atger in the early 19th century. Fragonard and Rubens are present, but the most beautiful are the 26 drawings by the great baroque Venetian Giambattista Tiepolo.

Jardin des Plantes
① 163 rue Auguste Broussonnet, T04 67 63 43 22, univ-montp1.fr. Jun-Sep Tue-Sun 1200-2000, Oct-May Tue-Sun 1200-1800.
This romantic, luxuriant 4.5-ha garden, beloved of artists and poets (Paul Valéry was a regular habitué) is the oldest botanical garden in France. It was founded in 1593 by Henri IV and laid out by Pierre Richer de Belleval, so the future doctors of France would know their medicinal plants.

Some of the trees here are unique, for example the massive Ginkgo biloba, the oldest of its kind in France, which has female branches grafted on to a male trunk. Don't miss the statue of Rabelais, with a motto on the back exhorting passersby to "live joyfully".

Musée Languedocien
① 7 rue Jacques Coeur, T04 67 52 93 03, musee-languedocien.com. Mid-Sep to mid-Jun Mon-Sat 1430-1730, mid-Jun to mid-Sep Mon-Sat 1500-1800, closed Sun and national holidays. €7, €4 student/child.
This museum is located in the Renaissance hôtel particulier of Jacques Coeur, the fabulously wealthy treasurer of Charles VII who, when charged with getting more taxes out of Languedoc, did so in a then-novel way, by investing in local projects so people would have more money in their pockets. That was until his downfall in 1451, when he was accused of poisoning the king's mistress.

The mansion was remodelled in the 17th century, when it was given the grandest staircase in Montpellier, but it still maintains Coeur's 'alchemist' coat of arms on a pillar and painted ceiling. Exhibits include prehistoric artefacts, Greek and Gallo-Roman finds, medieval paintings, ivories and sculpture, mule bridles from the Cévennes and an exceptional collection of ceramics, including some made in Montpellier.

Musée du Vieux Montpellier
① 1 place Pétrarque, T04 67 66 02 94. Tue-Sun 1030-1200 and 1330-1800. €3 (includes **Musée de l'Histoire de Montpellier**).
Installed in the beautiful Hôtel de Varennes, this five-room museum displays a hodgepodge of sculpture, religious artefacts (including the 13th-century statue of the Black Virgin that

once presided on the altar of Notre-Dame des Tables), prints, watercolours, plans, a model of the Bastille and the mallets for the *jeu de mail*, a 15th-century version of croquet played in Montpellier until the First World War.

Musée Fougau
① *Place Pétrarque, T04 67 84 31 58. Mid-Aug to mid-Jul Wed and Thu 1500-1800. €3.*
Fougau, means 'foyer' in Occitan, and this museum recreates an 18th-century apartment in the Hôtel de Varennes. It is furnished entirely by local donations and run by volunteers. There are some rare items (they have a jeu de mail) and frequent special exhibitions.

Musée de l'histoire de la France en Algérie (1830-1962)
① *Rue Joffre, due to open in early 2012.*
Hôtel Montcalm , the home of the general who lost the Battle of Quebec in 1759 is one of the last hôtel particuliers in Montpellier that still has its garden, and will feature photos, posters, architectural designs, models, paintings etc.

Beyond L'Ecusson

Antigone
From Place de la Comédie, walk through the shopping funnel that is Le Triangle to the ziggurat-style shopping centre **Polygone** (built in the early 1970s). There, you'll find yourself in former mayor Georges Frêche's most audacious project: the monumental, post-modern, neoclassical quarter of **Antigone**. Begun in 1983, it is a serenely classical antidote to Polygone's mercantile crassness.

On the map it looks like a key – a key to the future. '*Changer la ville pour changer la vie*' (Improve the city in order to improve life) was Frêche's motto, and he hired Barcelona architect Ricardo Bofill to build this pendant to l'Ecusson on 50 ha purchased from the army and the Church. Under Bofill's exaggerated cornices (set apart from the walls to provide views of the ever-changing sky), the goal was to create a humanist middle-income district. The place names – Place du Nombre d'Or (Golden Number Square), Place Marathon, Place Dionysos, etc – play on classic themes, as do the copies of famous Greek bronzes. Place du Millénaire celebrates Montpellier's first, and next, 1000 years.

Over the years, the trees have grown and amenities have been added along Antigone's 1.5-km axis, including the Mediathèque Federico Fellini with a library of 7000 films, the Mediathèque Emile Zola, the regional library and an Olympic-sized pool. Antigone reaches a grand finale with an enormous hemicycle, the **Esplande de l'Europe**, where a copy of the Victory of Samothrace presides over the banks of the Lez. On the far bank the vista is framed by the **Hôtel de Région**, Frêche's HQ as President of Languedoc-Roussillon. It's shaped like a glass arch, echoing the Grande Arche in Paris and reflecting the waters of the Lez.

Antigone is only the beginning of a master plan to expand Montpellier east of and along the Lez to the Mediterranean, and a new tram line is already in the works. One of the many projects already completed is the **Odysseum**, a 50-ha entertainment complex that includes a multiplex cinema, an ice skating rink, a planetarium and an aquarium. **Port Marianne** is an urban water sports centre just down from the Hôtel de Région, where a new town hall is planned along with the **Jardins de la Lironde**, a 21st-century garden city designed by Christian de Portzampac.

Aquarium Mare Nostrum

ⓘ *Odysseum, allée Ulysse, T04 67 13 05 50, aquariummarenostrum.fr. Sep-Jun daily 1000-1900, Jul-Aug daily 1000-2200. €15.50, €6 child (3-6), €11.50 child (7-12) under 3s free. Free parking, or take the tram (Line 1).*

Montpellier is proud of this huge state-of-the-art aquarium in the Odysseum leisure centre. Some 300 different marine species from sharks to penguins are on display, many in the 'balcony of the Ocean', one of the biggest and deepest pools in any aquarium. There's plenty for kids to enjoy, including an ice cave, a realistic cargo boat ride through a storm, and a simulated descent into an ocean abyss.

Parc Zoologique de Lunaret and La Serre Amazonienne

ⓘ *50 av d'Agropolis, T04 67 54 45 23, zoo.montpellier.fr. Easter- Oct Tue-Sun 1000-1830, Oct to Mar 0900-1700, closed Mon except national holidays. The zoo is free, the Serre Amazonienne is €6.50, €3 concession/child (6-18), under 6s free. To get there by public transport, take shuttle bus No 9 from the St-Eloi station (Tram 1).*

Montpellier's excellent zoo, north of the Ecusson, has a new attraction. Set up in conjunction with a park in Guyenne, the Amazonian greenhouse is dedicated to preserving endangered species (two-toed sloths, armadillos, ocelots) in mangroves, mountain forests, rainforest canopies and other specially reconstructed tropical environments.

Outside the city

Château de Flaugergues

ⓘ *1744 av Albert Einstein, T04 99 52 66 37, flaugergues.com. Jun-Jul, Sep Tue-Sun 1430-1830, otherwise by appointment. Park and gardens Mon-Sat 0930-1230 and 1430-1900, also Sun and national holidays in Jun, Jul, Sep 1430-1900. Guided tours of the interior €8.50, €6 concession. Park €6. For wine tastings, ring ahead. To get there by public transport, take Bus No 9 and get off at the Evariste Gallois stop.*

In the late 17th century, Montpellier's grandees built large summer residences or 'follies' in what was then the countryside. This château, begun in 1695 by Etienne de Flaugergues (advisor to the count of Montpellier), is the biggest of them all and is filled with 17th- and 18th-century furnishings, Flemish tapestries, ceramics and antique scientific and optical instruments. The park's box hedges and alleys are a fine example of 18th-century French gardens. The château's own AOC Coteaux du Languedoc is on sale in its caves.

Château de la Mogère

ⓘ *2235 rte de Vauguières, T04 67 65 72 01, lamogere.fr. Jun-Sep daily 1430-1830 (ring ahead on Sat), Oct-May Sat-Sun, national holidays 1430-1800. €5. Gardens open other days (but ring ahead).*

The Château de la Mogère, another of Montellier's grand follies, is located just southeast of the Odysseum. It was begun in 1719 and is set amid French gardens, massive cypresses and parasol pines. The owner, the Vicomte Gaston de Saporta, is often on hand to lead tours of the château's period furnishings, elegant plasterwork, paintings and family portraits. A lovely baroque *buffet d'eau* (a fountain built into a wall) overlooks the old kitchen garden.

L'Abbaye de Valmagne

ⓘ *On the D5, Villeveyrac, T04 67 78 06 09, valmagne.com. Easter-15 Jun Mon-Fri 1400-1800l Sat, Sun 1000-1800Mid-Jun to Sep daily 1000-1800, Oct to Easter daily 1400-1800; Guided tour and wine-tasting €7, €5.50 child, under 10s free.*

St Marie de Valmagne (40 km west of Montpellier) was founded in 1138 by Raymond Trencavel, Viscount of Béziers, Nîmes and Carcassonne. After joining the stricter Cistercian order in 1159 it became one of the most powerful abbeys in the region, growing so quickly that a new church was begun in 1257, modelled on the Gothic cathedrals in the Ile de France, with a 112-m nave just to contain the many monks. Valmagne soon became known for its parties rather than its piety, and in 1575 its own abbot switched over to the Protestant camp and led the attack against it. It limped on until the Revolution, when many of France's great religious houses were used as stone quarries – a fate Valmagne avoided by being converted into a winery in 1791.

Owned since 1838 by the descendants of the Count of Turenne, wine (AOC Coteaux du Languedoc and Grès de Montpellier) is still the abbey's main concern. The church, under its 24-m vaulted ceiling, is more lavish than the typically austere Cistercian edifice, and decorated (rather appropriately) with reliefs of vines. The cloister, planted with special Cistercian (Cîteaux) roses, has an utterly enchanting octagonal Gothic pavilion crowned with trellises, with a tall fountain in the centre. It's a lovely venue for the classical music festival in July and August.

Pézenas

In 1261, Louis IX purchased a down-at-heel former Roman colony called *Piscenae*, famous for its soft wool. In 1456 it became the seat of the governor and the Three Estates of Languedoc, making it the *de facto* regional capital before Louis XIV hustled the nobles and jurists off to Montpellier. Only princely Uzès can rival the old capital's streets of elegant *hôtels particuliers*, with their beautiful courtyards and external stairs. But Pézenas is proudest of Jean-Baptiste Poquelin, better known as Molière, whose company came to entertain the governor, the Prince of Conti, for three-month stints every summer from 1650-1656.

Musée de Vulliod-St-Germain

ⓘ *3 rue Albert-Paul Alliés, T04 67 98 90 59, ville-pezenas.fr. Jul-Oct Tue-Sun 1000-1200 and 1500-1900, Sep-Jun Tue-Sun 1000-1200 and 1400-1700.*

This magnificent *hôtel particulier* houses the kind of aristocratic accessories you might expect to find in Pézenas: 17th-century tapestries, ceramics, period furnishings and paintings, and items somewhat tenuously linking Molière to the town. Not surprisingly, the whole town was abuzz in June 2009 when the newest exhibit acquired by popular subscription finally arrived to take its place: Molière's Chair. When in Pézenas the playwright used to sit in the shop of his friend the barber, Gély (1 place Gambetta), and eavesdrop on conversations about local characters, inspiring at least two of his plays – *Dom Juan* and *Tartuffe*.

Scénovision Molière

ⓘ *Place des Etats-du-Languedoc, T04 67 98 35 39, scenovisionmoliere.com. Sep-Jun Mon-Sat 0900-1200 and 1400-1800, Sun 1000-1800, Jul-Aug 0900-1900, Wed and Fri 0900-1800, Jul-Aug 0900-2000. The last show is 1 hr 15 mins before closing. €7, €6 concession.*

Sharing the 17th-century Hôtel de Peyrat with the tourist office, this is a high-tech audiovisual evocation of Molière's life and work in five 'acts', ending with his death on stage while playing the *Malade Imaginaire* in Paris. Be warned, it's in French and the 3D glasses come in a comedy mask; you may feel silly but no one should recognize you.

Montpellier and around listings

For Sleeping and Eating price codes and other relevant information, see page 10.

🍴 Where to stay

Montpellier and around *p53*

€€€€ Baudon de Mauny, *1 rue de la Carbonnerie, T04 67 02 21 77, baudondemauny.com.* This extremely stylish B&B occupies an 18th-century *hôtel particulier* in the heart of Montpellier. In the same family for seven generations, the decor is a charming mix of old (including high ceilings, decorative stuccoes and an elegant stone staircase) and 21st-century design. There's Wi-Fi, a library and honesty bar with wines and spirits. Minimum stay two nights.

€€€€ Le Jardin des Sens, *11 av St-Lazare, just north of the centre, near the No 2 tram line, T04 99 58 38 38, jardindessens.com.* Although it presents an opaque façade, inside is a chic world full of contemporary art and colour. Clean lines dominate the decor of the 12 rooms, and there's a cosy living room and 11-m rooftop swimming pool. It is also attached to one of Montpellier's finest restaurants (see page 62).

€€€ Hôtel d'Aragon, *10 rue Baudin, T04 67 10 70 00, hotel-aragon.fr.* This newly renovated boutique hotel is only a few minutes' walk from the Place de la Comédie. The 12 air-conditioned rooms, each named after a famous author, are equipped with flat-screen satellite TVs and Wi-Fi. The stair to the upper two floors is a bit narrow, but the staff are very helpful with the bags. Breakfast, full of fresh goodies, is served in the glass-roofed veranda.

€€€ New Hotel du Midi, *22 bd Victor Hugo, T04 67 92 69 61, new-hotel.com/fr/hotel/du-midi.* By the Opéra Comédie, this belle époque institution was 'new' two centuries ago, but had a facelift in 2006. In spite of the busy location, the 44 rooms done up in chocolate, pistachio and raspberry tones are perfectly soundproofed. Discounts are

available in the nearby parking garage.

€€ Hôtel des Arts, *6 bd Victor Hugo, T04 67 58 69 20, hotel-des-arts.fr.* A simple but welcoming little hotel just off the Place de la Comédie. It offers en suite rooms in spring colours, all equipped with soundproofing, air conditioning, Wi-Fi and TV. There are also family rooms, which can sleep up to five. Prices are among the lowest in central Montpellier.

€€ Hôtel Le Guilhem, *18 rue Jean-Jacques Rousseau, T04 67 52 90 90, leguilhem.com.* Near the Faculté de Médecine and leafy Place de la Canorgue, Le Guilhem has 36 air-conditioned, peaceful rooms in a 16th-century house with a delightful garden. Note that standard doubles are in this price range, but others are more expensive. Children under 10 sharing their parents' room stay for free.

€€ Hôtel du Parc, *8 rue Achille Bégé, T04 67 41 16 49, hotelduparc-montpellier.com.* A favourite with romantics, this 18th-century *hôtel particulier* (a short stroll north of the historic centre) was the home of Count Vivier de Châtelard, and still has an aristocratic feel about it. There are 19 spacious air-conditioned rooms off a beautiful spiral stair. Breakfast is served on the sunny terrace and there's a free car park and Wi-Fi.

€€ Villa Juliette, *6 chemin de la Faissine, Pézenas, T04 67 35 25 38, villajuliette.com.* Overlooking Sans Souci Park and only a three-minute walk from the centre of Pézenas, this charming B&B in a 19th-century villa is a quiet little oasis in a Mediterranean garden with a curvaceous pool. There are five en suite rooms, and one room sleeps four to six people. If weather permits, breakfast is served in the garden.

€ Hôtel des Etuves, *24 rue des Etuves, T04 67 60 78 19, hoteldesetuves.fr.* On a peaceful pedestrian lane, 100 m from Place de la Comédie, this reliable budget choice has been in the same family for three generations. The 15 rooms are en suite and the continental breakfast is a bargain at €5.

€ Hôtel le Mistral, *25 rue Boussairolles, T04 67 58 45 25, hotel-le-mistral.com*. This little hotel, within easy walking distance of the train station, has been recently refurbished and is a good choice in a city where bargains are few and far between. Many rooms have a little balcony, and all come with flat-screen TVs and Wi-Fi. Parking is available nearby for €11 a day.

€ La Dordîne, *9 rue des Litanies, Pézenas, T04 67 90 34 81, ladordine.com*. This B&B in the heart of Pézenas is a medieval house with five simple but attractive rooms (ask for the 'Picpoul', with its views over the countryside). The young owners love wine and food and this is evident from the wine cellar, where you can go for a tasting, and from the superb breakfast of home-made cakes, breads, brioches, jams, fresh fruits and yoghurts. They also offer three newly renovated apartments

Self-catering

Appart'City Montpellier l'Orangerie, *29 bd Berthelot, T04 67 34 27 00, appartcity.com*. This new apartment hotel is on a quiet street south of the centre, but it's only 150 m from a No 2 tram stop. Each of the 147 studios and apartments comes with a kitchenette and comfortable sofa bed. Extra services include underground parking, laundry, buffet breakfast and broadband. Two days minimum stay; rates begin at €69 a night for two people.

Restaurants

Montpellier and around *p53*

€€€€ La Maison de la Lozère: Cellier-Morel, *27 rue de l'Aiguillerie, T04 67 66 46 36, celliermorel.com. Tue, Thu-Fri for lunch, Mon-Sat for dinner*. Eric Cellier and Pierre Morel captain this elegant restaurant in a 17th-century townhouse, where politicians take visiting VIPs, dining either under the pale stone vaults or in the plant-filled courtyard. The classy, inventive dishes on the frequently changing menu are served on undulating white plates; the desserts are unique (mint and ginger meringue) and over 550 wines fill the cellars. Fixed lunch menus start at €30; be sure to book.

€€€€ Le Jardin des Sens, *11 av St-Lazare, T04 99 58 38 38, jardindessens.com. Tue and Thu-Sat for lunch, Mon-Sat for dinner*. Twins Jacques and Laurent Pourcel serve their magnificent, creative cuisine in a stunning glass dining room in a Mediterranean garden. The ever-changing menu is based on the finest locally sourced ingredients, and features such things as soufflée de courgette blossoms with prawn tails, or caramelized duckling with pan-fried foie gras and cherries. There's a special dessert menu for chocolate lovers and excellent regional wines. Lunch menu €49.

€€€ La Réserve Rimbaud, *820 av St-Maur, T04 67 72 52 53, reserve-rimbaud.com. Tue-Fri and Sun for lunch, Mon-Sat for dinner*. In an idyllic setting on the Lez, this spot started out as a *guinguette* in 1835, and now boasts a fresh, contemporary look. Talented young chef Charles Fontès prepares regional delights such as delicious foie gras with date chutney, lamb from the Aveyron, and seafood *a la plancha*. Lunch menus start at €25; dinner, when it's at its most gorgeously romantic, is decidedly more at €60.

€€€ L'Entre Pots, *8 rue Louis Montagne, Pézenas, T04 67 90 00 00,. restaurantentrepots. com Tue-Sat for lunch and dinner*. The handsome, designer dining room is in a vaulted wine warehouse, and the main courses (scallop tempura, duck cooked in three different ways) couldn't be better. Add to that an excellent wine list, morish fruity desserts and lovely alfresco dining on the patio. Best to book. Lunch menus from €21, dinner menus from €29.

€€€ Le Pré St-Jean, *18 av du Mal-Leclerc, Pézenas, T04 67 98 15 31 restaurant-leprestjean.fr,. Tue- Sun for lunch, Tue- Sat for lunch*. Chef Philippe Cagnoli is a master of delicate, *mijotée* sauces that bring out the finest in the local oysters, mushrooms and other treats in this casual, chic, sunny restaurant. Excellent affordable wine list, too. Menus from €25; lunch €18.50.

€€€ Tamarillos, *2 place du Marché aux Fleurs, T04 67 60 06 00, tamarillos.biz. Daily for lunch and dinner.* After working with chef Guy Savoy, Philippe Chapon opened this restaurant drenched in colour. Appropriately for a cuisine that's based on fruit and flowers, it's in the city's old flower market. Think sea bass with a purée of herbs in a vanilla and lime sauce, a rose- and raspberry-flavoured cream dessert and gourmet coffees. Flower Power Plat du jour €14.

€€ Le Ban des Gourmands, *5 place Carnot, T04 67 65 00 85, bandesgourmands.com. Tue-Fri for lunch and dinner, Sat dinner.* This is a local favourite, with a friendly, informal, bistro atmosphere and fresh, market cuisine prepared with a Mediterranean flair. Vegetable lovers will enjoy chef Jacques Delépine's take on the seasonal harvest and the roast asparagus with lonza is delicious. The day's catch is perfectly prepared, and the succulent meats are sourced from one of Montpellier's top butchers.

€ La Pause Mermoz, *890 av Jean Mermoz, T04 99 54 65 19, lapause.unblog.fr. Mon-Fri 0730-1900.* A friendly, informal self-service just north of Antigone, with an all-you-can-eat lunch buffet for €10.90. The food is made fresh every morning and there are salads, crudités, charcuterie, mussels and delicious desserts as well.

€ L'Assiette aux Fromages, *17 rue Gustave, T04 67 58 94 48, assietteauxfromages.free.fr. Sep-Jul Mon-Fri for lunch and dinner, Mon-Sat for dinner.* The resolutely traditional decor, jovial informality and filling portions make this restaurant a firm favourite with families and groups of friends. Specializing in different styles of cheese fondue, it's especially popular in the cooler months. They also do salads and duck dishes.

€ Le Dilemme, *12 rue Farges, T04 67 69 02 13. Mon-Sun 1900-2400.* In the heart of Montpellier, Le Dilemme offers refined cuisine, a friendly ambiance and value for money. There's a wide range of choices – the 'dilemma' is deciding what to order. The foie gras with onion *confiture* is delectable, and (rare in France) the bread is home made. Set-price menus start at €14.

Cafés and bars

Cocco e Fragola, *8 rue de la Loge, place Jean-Jaurès, T04 67 02 03 28, coccoefragola.com. Mon-Fri and Sun 1200-2000, Sat 1200-2400.* Superb home-made Italian gelato, sorbets and smoothies, as well as fine Italian-style coffees, served in a luminous modern setting.

La Tavola da Pépé, *8 rue de l'Université, T04 67 02 19 25, tavoladapepe.fr. Tue-Sat 1900-0100.* This lively tapas bar stays open until the wee hours. A wide range of authentic tapas and seafood *a la plancha* accompany a choice of cocktails and wines.

Le Circus, *3 rue Collot, T04 67 60 42 05, www.circus-mtp.com. Open 1800-0100.* A trendy New York-style bar with a cool, colourful circus theme and reasonable prices. It's a favourite place to start or end an evening out.

Le Huit, *8 rue de l'Aiguillerie, T06 60 80 91 17, facebook.com/lehuit. Tue-Sat 1800-0100.* Hip 20-somethings flock to this late-night bar for the cocktails and the music – alternative, pop, rock, funk, etc. Frequent live performances.

Morceau de la Lune, *14 rue du Pila St-Gély, T04 67 52 80 59, restaurant-morceau-de-lune. fr. Wed-Fri 1200-1400; Tue-Sat 1900-2300.* A romantic wine bar/restaurant on a pedestrian street near Place de la Comédie, Morceau de la Lune serves seasonal, contemporary dishes to go with its 200 different wines, mostly from Languedoc. Bottles range from €14-95; they also do wine-tasting evenings.

Montpellier and around *p53*
Cinema
Cinéma Gaumont Comédie, *10
place de la Comédie, T08 92 69 66 96,
cinemasgaumontpathe.com.* A central, eight-
screen complex showing new releases.

Clubs
JAM (Jazz Action Montpellier), *100 rue
Ferdinand de Lessps, T04 67 58 30 30, lejam.
com.* Montpellier's jazz club is a local
institution and puts on several concerts a
week from October to July. It's south of the
centre, off Avenue Près d'Arènes.
Bellano, *Le Grand Travers, La Grande-Motte,
T06 67 90 46 59, bellano.fr Apr-Oct, Thu-Sat
2300-0600.* Huge Ibiza-style venue that
attracts clubbers across Languedoc.
La Villa Rouge, *Rte Palavas, Lattes, take
the Montpellier Sud exit off the A9, T04 67 06
50 54, la-villarouge.fr. Thu-Sat from 0100.*
Massive gay/straight techno club.
Le Cargo, *5 rue du Grand St-Jean, T04 67 29
96 85, cargo-montpellier.fr. Sep-Jun Tue-Thu
2000-0200, Fri-Sat 2000-0500.* Music bar/
disco aimed at the university set, with plenty
of salsa and merengue on Tuesdays. Free
entry weekdays, on weekends it's free until
midnight.
Le Rockstore, *20 rue de Verdun, T04 67 06
80 00, rockstore.fr.* A red Cadillac pierces the
façade of central Montpellier's rock temple,
founded in 1986 and still going strong.
There are frequent concerts, discos, DJs, etc.
The bar opens at 2000.

Gay and lesbian
Café de la Mer, *5 place du Marché aux Fleurs,
T04 67 60 79 65.* Montpellier's first gay bar
with its big sunny terrace is an institution. It's
a great place to meet up and find out what's
on in the city.
Le Men's, *26 rue de Candolle, T04 67 66 21
95, facebook.com/lemens daily Tue-Sun 1900-
0100.* Montpellier has a lively gay scene, and
this glamorous tapas restaurant, bar and
club spread out over five rooms with DJs
from across France is a favourite rendezvous.

Music and theatre
Corum, *Esplanade Charles de Gaulle, T04
67 61 67 61, enjoy-montpellier.com.* This
contemporary conference centre also
houses the Berlioz Opera, famed for its
cutting-edge acoustics.
Le Zénith Sud, *Domaine de Grammont,
Montpellier Est exit off the A9, T04 67 64 50
00, enjoy-montpellier.com.* Modelled on
Le Zénith in Paris, this is the venue for big
names on tour (Arctic Monkeys, Sting, St
Petersburg Ballet).
Opéra Comédie, *Place Molière, T04 67
60 19 99, opera-montpellier.com.* Classic
repertory performed by the Opéra National
Montpellier Languedoc-Roussillon.

Montpellier and around *p53*
The Ecusson is full of boutiques and
fascinating little shops. Rue de la Loge is
the high street, but side streets such as Rue
St-Guilhem and Rue de l'Ancien Courrier
are also full of treasures. The medieval lanes
around St-Anne are the place to look for
quirky shops and antiques.

Arts and antiques
Boutique 110 Volts, *24 rue de la
Mediterranée, T06 81 95 86 13, 110volts.net.
Mon-Fri 0930-1215 and 143-1900.* Fun shop
selling household items and accessories
from the 1950s-1970s.

Clothing and accessories
Boutique Patricia Orssaud, *16 rue de
l'Argenterie, T04 67 66 04 47, boutique-
patricia-orssaud.fr. Mon 1430-1900, Tue-Sat
1000-1900.* Elegant clothes for women by
top French and Italian designers.
Diplodocus, *1 rue Valedeau, T04 67 02 72 50,
diplodocus.fr. Mon 1400-1900, Tue-Sat 1000-
1900.* Women's clothing, aimed at the over
30s, with an emphasis on natural fabrics

from silk to cashmere.

Erbe, *19bis rue de la Loge, T04 67 54 97 65. Mon -Sat 1000-1900.* Stylish, mostly Italian and Spanish shoes for men and women.

Food and drink

La Maison Régionale des Vins, *34 rue St-Guilhem, T04 67 60 40 41. Mon 1000-2000, Mon-Sat 0930-2000.* Excellent range of Languedocien wines and spirits and everything that goes with them.

Les Halles Castellane, *Rue de la Loge, T04 67 66 29 92. Mon-Sat 0730-1930, Sun 0700-1400.* Montpellier's wonderful covered market.

Pinto, *14 rue de l'Argenterie, T04 67 60 57 65, pinto.fr. Mon 1430-1900, Tue-Sat 0845-1230 and 1430-1900.* For over 50 years Pinto has been selling both world and regional products, including Montpellier's 17th-century *Délice des Trois Grâces* dark chocolate with a touch of ginger and spice.

Puig Valero, *5 bis place Laissac, T04 67 58 02 38. Tue-Sat 0700-1300 and 1600-1930.* Perfect *fromages*; a must for any cheese lover.

Music

Comptoir du Disque, *2 place Pétrarque, T04 67 60 91 71, lecomptoirdudisque.fr. Mon 1400-1900, Tue-Sat 1100-1300 and 1400-1700.* Extraordinary selection of over 150,000 vinyl records.

Toys

Pomme de Reinette, *35 rue de l'Aiguillerie, T04 67 60 52 78, .tradition-jouet.com. Mon 1400-1900, Tue-Fri 1000-1230 and 1400-1900, Sat 1000-1900.* A fascinating labyrinth filled with vintage toys and museum pieces, as well as all kinds of games, music boxes, models and much, much more.

Pezenas *p60*
Food and drink

Percheron, *41 cours Jean Jaurès,, T 04 67 98 13 32. Tue-Sat 0900-1230 and 1500-1900, Sun 0800-12.30.* Come here to buy Pézenas' sweet/savoury speciality, *petits pâtés de Pézenas.* The recipe was given to the town

as a gift in the 18th century by the Indian Viceroy Lord Clive, who brought his chef along on holiday.

What to do

Montpellier and around *p53*
Children

La Forêt d'Acrobates, *Base de Bessilles, Motagnac, T06 07 13 43 80, loisirs-foret. com.* Some 90 activities, including Tarzan jumps and zip wires, in the forest that once belonged to the Abbaye de Valmagne. From ages three and up.

Golf

Golf de Coulondres, *72 rue des Erables, St-Gély-du-Fesc, T04 67 84 13 75, coulondres. com.* Five minutes north of Montpellier, a beautiful piney 18-hole par 73 course. Also a nine-hole compact course.

Golf de Montpellier Massane, *Baillargues, T04 67 87 87 87, massane.com.* Resort complex with an undulating 18-hole par 72 course, a nine-hole pitch and putt course and a spa for non golfers.

Ice skating

Vegapolis, *Quartier Odysseum, T04 99 52 26 00, vert-marine.com.* France's first ice-skating rink devoted to fun, complete with disco music and lights. You can rent skates as well.

Water sports

Piscine Olympique d'Antigone, *195 av Jacques Cartier, T04 67 15 63 00, montpellier-agglo.com.* Montpellier's biggest indoor pool has giant slides, rapids etc as well as lanes for serious swimmers. It's near both tram lines.

Transport

Montpellier and around *p53*
Montpellier's historic centre, L'Ecusson, is the biggest pedestrian zone in France. Car parks and garages are signposted on the periphery, especially on the south side and

towards Antigone. There are cheaper car parks along the city's two tramlines. The city's two tramlines are **Hirondelles** (Line 1) and **Fleurs** (Line 2); the future Line 3, **Haute Couture** (designed by Christian Lacroix) will go as far as Lattes-Pérols and the sea. Tickets cost €1.40 (€2.50 return) and are valid for one hour on both buses and trams; a day pass is €3.50 From Thursday to Saturday (2400-0500), Amigo buses provide a service which runs from Gare St-Roch to the nightclubs (for timetables, see **Transports de l'Agglomération de Montpellier** TaM, T04 67 22 87 87, montpellier-agglo.com).

The **Vélomagg** scheme allows you to hire a bicycle in one of 50 locations. It costs €1 for up to four hours or €2 for a day.

There are taxi ranks at the train station and in Place de la Comédie; alternatively, ring T04.67 03 20 00.

The train station is Gare St-Roch, a five-minute walk south of the Place de la Comédie, T36 35. The bus station is on Rue du Grand-St-Jean, 200 m from the train station, T04 67 92 01 43.

Directory

Montpellier and around *p53*

Money Banque Populaire, 11 place de la Comédie; BNP Paribas, 8 rue Maguelone. ATM. **Medical services** Hospital: **CHU-Hôpital Lapeyronie**, 191 avenue Doyen-Gaston-Giraud, T04 67 33 67 33. Pharmacy: De la Comédie, 1 rue Verdun, T04 67 58 54 94 ; Foch, 20 rue Foch, T04 67 60 69 23. **Post office** 15 rue Rondelet, T04 6702 28 68. **Tourist information** 30 allée Jean de Lattre de Tassigny, T04 67 60 60 60, ot-montpellier.fr (Jul-Sep Mon-Fri 0900-1930, Sat, Sun and national holidays 0930-1800, Sun and national holidays; Oct-Jun Mon-Sat 100-1800, Sun and holidays 1000-1700). Save money by purchasing a **City Card** at the tourist office for 24, 48 or 72 hours (€13, €21, €27, half price for children). It offers free transport, guided tours and free or reduced entry to Montpellier's main sites. The tourist office also offers two-hour guided tours (€8) every Wednesday, Saturday and Sunday at 1430 (1700 in summer); reservations essential, T04 67 60 19 27. These are your only chance to see inside the Arc de Triomphe, the Faculté de Médecine or the Mikveh (Jewish ritual baths).

Inland from Montpellier

This is classic *garrigue* country, green with aromatic scrub, and even the wines produced here have a certain earthy herbal essence. West and north of Montpellier, the *garrigue* is steeply sliced by rivers and otherworldly caves and gorges and dotted with medieval churches, including two famous ones along the road to Compostela.

Le Pic St-Loup and St-Martin-de-Londres

At 644 m, Le Pic St-Loup is one of the great landmarks of the *garrigue* – a bluish limestone ridge that from certain angles appears to come to a needle-sharp point. It's the centrepiece and namesake of a small but emerging wine region, the northernmost pocket of the Coteaux du Languedoc. In the Middle Ages it signalled to pilgrims en route to Compostela that they were approaching St-Martin-de-Londres; this is the French for London, but it's also the Celtic word for the now dry swamp that surrounded this pretty village. St-Martin-de-Londres was built over a prehistoric settlement and named after a handsome church founded in the time of Charlemagne in a picture-perfect setting, encircled by old stone houses in an exquisite, arcaded medieval square. Part of the ensemble once belonged to a priory set up by the Abbaye de Gellone, the pilgrims' next major stop.

St-Guilhem-le-Désert and around

A pilgrimage destination even before Compostela, St-Guilhem-le-Désert is a gem of a honey-stoned village with narrow cobbled lanes and flower-filled balconies surrounding a World Heritage Site abbey. Just don't visualize sand and palms – the 'desert' in its name means deserted. Be warned though, in summer and at weekends it's anything but.

L'Abbaye de Gellone

ⓘ *Place de la Liberté, T04 67 57 44 33, st-guilhem-le-desert.com. Cloisters and church daily outside of mass, 0800-1200 and 1300-1800. Museum Oct-Apr Sat, Sun, French school and national holidays 1300-1700, May-Sep Mon-Sat 1030-1200 and Mon-Sun 1300-1800,. (including audio guide) €2.50.*

Guilhem, Count of Toulouse and grandson of Charles Martel, was one of the great paladins of his cousin Charlemagne. He defeated a large Saracen army led by Hisham I near Narbonne and liberated Barcelona in 803; some say he captured Orange as well. In gratitude, Charlemagne gave Guilhem a piece of the True Cross and he retired here in 804, founding an abbey of Gellone (the old name of the River Hérault) under the spiritual guidance of his friend, St Benedict of Aniane. Soon after his death he was canonized and pilgrims began to arrive, including the very first Crusaders to the Holy Land; other pilgrims flowed in from Spain. In 1050, the great abbey church was built in the Lombard style, decorated with blind arcading, notably around its splendid apse, and in 1066 Guilhem was canonized again – a rare honour. The tower was added in the 14th century; the huge plane tree in the charming Place de la Liberté was planted in 1855.

Once again home to a community of monks, Guilhem's abbey is sombre and beautiful. It has been stripped of much of its original decoration: its reliquaries, saintly sarcophagus and once-famous library were sacked by the Protestants during the Wars of Religion, and its cloister was sold in the early 20th century to the Cloisters Museum in New York. There are traces of frescoes, and fragments of the capitals and other stonework in the refectory museum, as well as a film on the missing cloister. The best time to hear the 18th-century organ is during the July Festival of Baroque Organ and Choral Music.

Pont du Diable and La Maison du Grand Site

ⓘ *Aniane, T04 67 57 58 83, saintguilhem-valleeherault.fr. Maison du Grand Site open Apr-Jun, Sep, Oct 1030-1800; Jul & Aug 1000-1930.*

Three kilometres south of St-Guilhem, the road parallels the Pont du Diable, the spectacular bridge built in the 11th century to help pilgrims over the Gorges de L'Hérault. To take a good look or to picnic or swim, park by the Maison du Grand Site where there's a tourist office, a shop selling local products and wines and a brasserie, as well as a free shuttle to St-Guilhem-le-Désert.

Grotte de Clamouse

ⓘ *Between St-Jean-de-Fos and St-Guilhem-le-Désert, T04 67 57 71 05, grottedeclamouse. com. Nov-Jan Sat and Sun 1430 and 1600; Feb-May and Oct 1030-1620, Jun and Sep 1030-1720, Jul-Aug 1030-1820. €9, €7.70 (12-18) €5.50 child (4-12), under 4s free.*
At a constant 15°C even in August, this living cave is one of the most beautiful in France. It has recently been fitted with LED lighting and music, and a video explains its history and geography. One highlight is the Cathedral of Time with a pair of giant stalagmite 'organs'; another is the glittering White Corridor of spiky aragonite crystals.

Prieuré St-Michel-de-Grandmont

ⓘ *Soumont (west of St-Guilhem, towards Lodève), T04 67 44 09 31, prieure-grandmont.fr. Priory and Megalithic park 5 Feb-Dec 25 1000-1800 Guided tours Oct to Apr Tue-Sat 1030 and 1500, May-Sep 1030, 1500, 1600 and 1700. €10.*
This 13th-century priory, which frequently hosts concerts of medieval music, has an animal park and grand views down to the sea, but the site is also essential viewing for anyone who loves Neolithic megaliths. The star is the spectacular 2-m-high **Dolmen Coste-Rouge** (c 2000 BC), with a unique 'oven door'.

Ganges and the Upper Hérault

A market town at the confluence of the Rieutord, Vis and Hérault rivers, Ganges offers a good base for exploring the northern *garrigue*. People come to canoe down the gorges of the Hérault from the little fortified village of **Laroque** (just to the south) or **St-Bauzille-de-Putois** (just to the north); walk along the watermill-lined 13th-century irrigation canal at *Cazilhac*; or swim in the waterfalls of the Vis at **St-Laurent-du-Minier**. They also come to see two tremendous holes in the ground: the Grotte des Demoiselles and the Cirque de Navacelles.

Grotte des Demoiselles

ⓘ *St-Bauzille-de-Putois, T04 67 73 70 02, demoiselles.com. Tours Nov-Feb Mon-Sat 1400-1600, Sun and French school holidays 1000-1600, Mar and Oct Sun and French national holidays 1000-1630, Apr, May-Jun Mon-Sat 1000-1730, Sun and French school holidays 1000-1730, Jul-Aug daily 1000-1800. €9.50, €7.50 young person (12-17), €6.50 child (6-11), €1.50 child (3-5).*
A funicular does the hard work, taking visitors to the entrance of this spectacular stalactite cave, the legendary home of beautiful fairies, the *demoiselles*. The cave also has a long local history as a hideout for the Protestants in the early 18th-century War of the Camisards, and for priests during the Revolution.

Cirque de Navacelles

You'll begin to wonder if the signs are pulling your leg as you follow them up to a vast empty stretch of *causse*, and then suddenly, breathtakingly there it is yawning at your feet: a spectacular canyon, where the limestone has been carved over millions of years by the tight meander of the River Vis. After drinking in the views from the tops of the cliffs (**St-Maurice Navacelles** has the best views, and a restaurant) take the winding drive down to **Navacelles**, the sweet little village that from high above resembles an island on the canyon floor, where you can jump off the rocks into the cool waterfall.

Inland from Montpellier listings

For Sleeping and Eating price codes and other relevant information, see page 10.

🛏 Where to stay

Inland from Montpellier *p67*
€€ Hôtel le Guilaume d'Orange, *2 av Guilaume d'Orange, St-Guilhem-le-Désert, T04 67 57 24 53, guilhaumedorange.com.* Book early and bag one of the 10 delightful spacious rooms in this stylish hotel built of old stone. The decor of each is well thought out, with light natural tones and a mix of antiques. Owner Aurore is very helpful and also runs an excellent restaurant shaded by ancient plane trees.
€€ Hotel Les Norias, *254 av des Deux Ponts, Cazilhac, Ganges, T04 67 73 55 90, les-norias. fr.* Peace and quiet is guaranteed at this ivy-covered former silk mill. With 11 rooms, it is set in a lush park on the banks of the Hérault and there's a restaurant and even a private beach for dips in the river.

Restaurants

Inland from Montpellier *p67*
€€€€ Les Muscardins, *19 rte des Cévennes, St-Martin-de-Londres, T04 67 55 75 90, les-muscardins.fr. Wed-Sun for lunch and dinner.* Founded by chef Georges Rousset and now run by his son, Thierry, Les Muscardins draws gourmet pilgrims up from Montpellier to feast on succulent Aubrac beef and shallots, with a parsnip purée and *ravioli à la truffe blanche d'Alba*. This and other more exotic avant-garde dishes are matched by a superb wine cellar. Fixed price lunch menu €27. Be sure to book.
€€€ La Cour, *Mas de Baumes, Ferrières-les-Verreries, T04 66 80 88 80, oustaldebaumes. com. Open Wed-Sun for lunch and dinner.* Located east of St-Bauzille-de-Putois, this is a delightful haven of peace and quiet in an old stone farm, with views of the Pic St Loup.

Chef Eric Tapié varies his menu according to season: in autumn try the mouth-watering risotto with cèpes, and pigeon with figs and pan-fried foie gras. Vegetarians are well catered for as well. Menus from €29, and they have lovely rooms so you don't have to drive home.
€€€ Restaurant de Lauzan, *3 bd de l'Esplanade, Gignac (south of St-Guilhem-le-Désert), T04 67 57 50 83, restaurant-delauzun. com. Tue-Fri for lunch and dinner, Sat for dinner, Sun for lunch.* Young Matthieu de Lauzun studied under Michel Bras and prepares gorgeous dishes on the palette of black and white plates in this modern, no-nonsense shrine to food. Try the slow-cooked pork, the seafood marinated in lime juice or his own version of Sète's *bourride*. The *cave* is first rate. A €21 *formule* is served weekdays.
€€ Le Mas de Coulet, *Rte de Montpellier, Brissac (2.5 km south of St-Bauzille-de-Putois), T04 67 83 72 43, masdecoulet.com. Oct-Mar Fri for dinner, Sat for lunch and dinner, Sun for lunch, Apr-Jun and Sep Thu-Sat for lunch and dinner, Sun-Tue for lunch, Jul-Aug daily for lunch and dinner.* In a peaceful rural setting, this restaurant serves hearty simple dishes such as onion tart, grilled lamb chops and delicious *salades composées* with duck, plus some you don't see often such as *joues de porc à l'ancienne* (pork cheeks). Set menus from €24-35. They also have pretty rooms (€€) and gîtes with a pool.

Shopping

Inland from Montpellier *p67*
Mas de Daumas Gassac, *D32, Aniane (south of St-Guilhem), T04 67 57 88 45, daumas-gassac.com. Sep-Jun Mon-Sat 1000-1200 and 1400-1800, Jul-Aug daily 0930-1830.* One of the most famous vineyards in Languedoc, owned by Aimé Guibert who featured in the film *Mondovino*. The wines are organic and

the grapes hand-picked. They also sell olive oil and vinegar.

What to do

Inland from Montpellier *p67*
Canoeing
Canoe Rapido, *Rue St-Benôit d'Aniane, St-Guilhem-le-Désert, T04 67 55 75 75, st-guilhem-le-desert.com/canoe-rapido.html.* Canoe or kayak 12 km down the gorge of the Hérault.
Canoë Le Moulin, *Laroque and St-Bauzille-de-Putois, T04 67 75 30 73, canoelemoulin.*

fr. Canoe Le Moulin has two bases for paddling down the Hérault. Trips run from 4 April to 15 October and last from one to 48 hours (they provide tents for longer trips).

Golf
Fontcaude, *Rte de Lodève (direction Millau), Juvignac, T04 67 45 90 00, golfhotelmontpellier.com.* Near St-Guilhem-le-Désert, an 18-hole par 72 course, plus a nine-hole par 29 'executive course' in the *garrigue*; there's also a hotel and restaurant.

Coastal Hérault

Lined with big lagoons and sandy beaches, the Hérault's long stretch of sea shore is full of surprises: there's La Grande-Motte, a cross between the 1964 New York World's Fair and a Babylonian ziggurat, and Le Cap d'Adge, a colony founded by the ancient Greeks, who would probably approve that half of the beaches are for naturists. Although the main Montpellier beach, Palavas, is low on charm, there's Maguelone (the 'cathedral of the sands'), Roman mosaics, dinosaur eggs, lagoons full of shellfish and the salty, lively Sète.

Montpellier's coast

La Grande Motte

This easternmost end of the Hérault coast was always known as the 'Big Lump', and the name stuck in 1963, when the French decided to make this grassy knoll into the seaside resort of the future. Architect Jean Balladur (brother of former Prime Minister Eduard Balladur) took charge, designated a 'Point Zero' and radiated out from there, presenting the French with (what seemed at the time) a dream of the future, full of 1960s go-go panache: brightly coloured curving holiday flats, ziggurat hotels, groovy shopping plazas, a casino, a thalassotherapy spa, and golf courses and tennis courts galore on the sandy beaches. It was a huge hit, and it still is. It's kept gleaming and is busy all year round, intermingled with 43,000 trees, pedestrian walkways and a huge marina.

Cathédrale de Maguelone

ⓘ *From Villeneuve-lès-Mageulone, cross the bridge from the car park (€4) and walk 2 km around the Etang de l'Arnel. In summer there's a free train to the cathedral and beaches, for information T04 67 50 63 63, compagnons-de-maguelone.org. Open 1000-1800.*

The roots of Montpellier lie in Maguelone, a thin vine-covered volcanic strip linked to the mainland by a causeway. Originally a Phoenician or Etruscan trading post, it became a Visigoth bishopric, one of the seven cities of Septimania. The sixth-century cathedral was rebuilt in the 11th century, part church and part fortress against marauding pirates.

Pirates, however, weren't as deadly as the tensions between Catholics and Protestants during the Reformation. In 1536, the bishop moved to higher ground in Montpellier, leaving the town of Maguelone to become a Protestant stronghold. In 1622, Richelieu ordered it razed to the ground to keep them from ever coming back – except for this church, which was left evocatively alone amid the vines on a lido. It's an austere place, relieved only by the scene over the door showing Christ and the Four Evangelists, some sculpted capitals and tombs. You can climb the bell tower for the view. Another reason to visit is Maguelone's beach, which is lovely and rarely crowded even in summer, except during its prestigious June festival of medieval and baroque music.

Sète and the Bassin de Thau

Squeezed on a narrow strip between sea and lagoon, Sète is a likable, salty port that works and parties hard. It was founded in 1666 by Colbert, Louis XIV's powerful finance minister, who saw that the new Canal du Midi needed a proper seaport, and that this hill on a sandy strip along the Bassin de Thau provided a perfect, defensible site. To encourage people to move here, Colbert showed them what was possible by building a fake city out of wood and cardboard. The ploy worked, and a real Sète was soon built, a town that calls itself the 'Venice of Languedoc' for its many canals. Vibrant festivals fill the summer calendar, and the unusual museums are fun. Sète's speciality is a unique snack called a tielle sètoise, a pie filled with a delicious mix of cuttlefish, onion and tomato.

Musée International des Arts Modestes

ⓘ *23 quai du Maréchal de Lattre de Tassigny, T04 99 04 76 44, miam.org. Oct-Mar Wed-Mon 1000-1200 and 1400-1800, Apr-Sep daily 0930-1200 and 1400-1800. €5, €2 young person/child (10-18).*

'Modest Arts' are everyday knick-knacks and gadgets that make you smile, whether they are mass-produced or a one-off. This delightfully kitch museum is run by artist-brothers Richard and Hervé Di Rosa (inventors in the 1980s of Figuration Libre, an art influenced by comic books), who display treasures accumulated over the past three decades in an organized chaos. It's fun for kids and adults and there are frequent special exhibits on Elvis and other kitsch-magnets.

Musée Paul Valéry

ⓘ *Rue François Desnoyer, T04 99 04 76 16, museepaulvalery-sete.fr. Apr-Oct Wed-Mon 0930-1900, Nov-Mar Wed-Mon 1000-1800. €5, €2 young person/child (10-18).*

Sète's poet and scientist Paul Valéry (1871-1945) wrote one of his most famous poems about the Cimetière Marin, adjacent to this museum on the steep slopes of Mont St Clair. Besides 18th- to 20th-century paintings by such artists as Courbet, Jongkind, Desnoyer and Sarthou, there are exhibitions of contemporary works and frequent special exhibitions. Other rooms are dedicated to Valéry's life and art and to the *Joutes Nautiques*, with paintings and models, costumes and attempts to explain the rules, which vary from city to city.

Espace Brassens

ⓘ *67 bd Camille Blanc, T04 99 04 76 26, espace-brassens.fr. Jun and Sep daily 1000-1200 and 1400-1800, Oct-May Tue-Sun 1000-1200 and 1400-1800, Jul-Aug daily 1000-1200 and 1400-1900. €5, €2 young person/child (10-18), under 10s free.*

A short drive west of the centre along the Corniche de Neuburg, this homage to Georges Brassens (1921-1981) is a must for lovers of *la chanson française*. Brassens was a beloved chansonnier/songwriter/poet and a sometime bad boy who was born in Sète. An audio tour tells the story of his life and music, including a video of his 1972 concert in Paris.

Around the Bassin de Thau

The largest and deepest of all Languedoc's coastal *étangs*, the Basin de Thau is a famous nursery for oysters and 17 other kinds of shellfish. On weekends and summer evenings its seafood restaurants, which tend to be better and cheaper than the more touristy offerings in Sète, are packed. Try one in **Bouzigues**, a pocket-sized port synonymous with some of France's best oysters, which has spectacular views of the oyster beds – neat rows of wooden tables set in the water like a vast mermaid restaurant. Or head to calmer **Mèze** to the west, or pretty **Marseillan**, a sweet fishing village at the beginning of the Canal du Midi, where the Bassin de Thau has a channel to the sea.

La Villa Loupian

ⓘ *Loupian (4.5 km west of Bouzigues), T04 67 18 68 18, ccnbt.fr/ccnbt-richesse-patrimoine-vestiges-archeologiques-musee-villa-loupian. Sep-Jun Wed-Mon 1330-1800, Jul-Aug daily 1330-1900, last admission 1700. €4.60, €3.05 student.*

Located along the Via Domitia, this luxurious Gallo-Roman villa, inhabited from the first century BC to the sixth century AD, was subject to a 30-year excavation. The patrician owners (whose initials were MAF) owned a vast tract of vines, and a pottery that made the amphoras used to import their wine across the Mediterranean. In the fourth century the villa was rebuilt with lavish mosaic floors, attributed to Syrian artists. Visits include the museum and a guided tour of the villa, now sheltered under a large roof. There are free guided tours most days at 1100.

Musée Parc des Dinosaures

ⓘ *Mèze, T04 67 43 02 80, musee-parc-dinosaures.com. Feb-Jun and Sep daily 1400-1800, Jul-Aug daily 1000-1900, Oct-Dec daily 1400-1700, Jan Sat-Sun 1400-1700. €8.70, €7.20 child (5-12).*

Kids love this place. The park features life-sized models of dinosaurs (including a 25-m brachiosaurus, said to be largest skeleton in the world) in a 5-ha park, where clutches of dinosaur eggs and other fossils were discovered in the 1990s.

Noilly Prat

ⓘ *Marseillan Port, T04 67 77 20 15, noillyprat.com. Mar-Apr, Oct-Nov Mon-Sat 1000-1200 and 1430-1730, May-Sep 1000-1200 and 1430-1900. €3.50, €2 young person/child (12-18), under 12s free, family €7.*

The straw-coloured Noilly Prat, the 'Rolls Royce of Vermouths' and one of France's distinctive tipples, has been distilled in Marseillan since 1813. This popular guided tour takes you through the manufacturing process, which includes leaving wooden casks of wine out in the sun for a year.

Agde and Le Cap d'Agde

Founded near the mouth of the Hérault by the Greeks in the fifth century BC, *Agathé Tyché* (Good Fortune) was an important ancient port of call for ships sailing between Italy and Spain. Rebuilt in the Middle Ages, the old town of Agde looks like no other town in France. Positioned on top of a volcanic bubble, its buildings are made of blocks of black basalt, including the rugged 12th-century fortress of a church, the **Cathédrale de Saint-Etienne**, built over a Temple of Diana.

Le Cap d'Agde, Agde's modern beach-lined resort extension, draws a large contingent of Parisian fashion victims. A large swathe of land and beach is given over to the biggest (discreetly fenced) naturist resort in Europe. If it's all too busy though, head to dreamy, dune-tufted **La Tamarissière**, shaded by a 200-year-old pine forest, just west at the mouth of the Hérault.

Musée de l'Ephèbe

ⓘ *Mas de la Clape, Le Cap d'Agde, T04 67 94 69 60, capdagde.com. Nov-Mar Mon, Wed-Sat 0900-1200 and 1400-1700, Sun 1400-1700, Sep-Oct and Mar-Jun Mon, Wed-Sat 0900-1200 and 1400-1800, Sun 1400-1800, Jul-Aug Mon-Fri 0900-1915, Sat-Sun 1200-1900. €4.70, €3.60 senior, €1.80 young person/child (10-18), under 10s free.*

This excellent museum, built in 1984 near the port, was the first in France dedicated to underwater archaeology, and the nearby seas and river have yielded some choice finds. On display is an ornate Etruscan bronze tripod, one of only five ever found, and a bronze Eros and 'royal child' (identified as the son of Caesar and Cleopatra), both discovered in 2001.

The prize, however, is a Hellenistic bronze of a youth (*ephèbe*), identified as a young Alexander the Great, discovered in 1964 in the Hérault. There's also a vast collection of amphoras, pots, anchors, marbles and remains of ancient ships and finds from more recent wrecks, up to the 19th century.

Musée Agathois

ⓘ *5 rue de la Fraternité, Le Cap d'Agde, T04 67 94 82 51 capdagde.com. Nov-Mar Mon, Wed-Sat 0900-1200 and 1400-1700, Sun 1400-1700, Sep-Oct Mar-Jun Mon, Wed-Sat 0900-1200 and 1400-1800, Sun 1400-1800, Jul-Aug Mon-Fri 0900-1915, Sat-Sun 1200-1900. €4.70, €3.60 senior, €1.80 young person/child (10-18), under 10s free.*

Housed in a Renaissance *hôtel particulier*, this surprisingly large collection covers the history of Agde from medieval times to the present day. There are costumes, lace, headdresses, furnishings, paintings and more.

Coastal Hérault listings

For Sleeping and Eating price codes and other relevant information, see page 10.

🛏 Where to stay

Coastal Hérault *p73*

€€€ Hôtel Méditerranée, *277 allée du Vaccarès, La Grande-Motte, T04 67 56 53 38, hotellemediterranee.com*. If you belong to the half of humanity that adores La Grande-Motte, this 40-room hotel is the place to stay. The building, set in a pretty Mediterranean garden 200 m from the beach, dates from 1960s but has recently been handed over to local artists who have frescoed and decorated the rooms with imagination, colour and panache. The pool, hamman and restaurant-bar are added bonuses.

€€€ Le Grand Hôtel, *17 quai de Tassigny, Sète, T04 67 74 71 77, legrandhotelsete. com*. Classy and centrally located, this hotel is full of the 19th-century charm of the bourgeoisie and there's a wonderful iron and glass patio by the lobby. Near the bottom of this price range, it offers airy, pastel, air-conditioned rooms with Wi-Fi. There's a huge breakfast buffet for €10 and use of a garage for €9.

€ Hôtel Venezia, *Les Jardins de la Mer, 20 La Corniche de Neuburg, Sète, T04 67 51 39 38, hotel-sete.com*. This hotel, run by friendly Christophe and his parents, is only 50 m from the beach. It offers 18 en suite rooms that can sleep up to four, each with a balcony. There's also free parking and Wi-Fi, too.

Restaurants

Coastal Hérault *p73*

€€ Chez Philippe, *20 rue de Suffren, Marseillan, T04 67 01 70 62. Mid-Feb to May and Sep to mid-Nov Wed-Sun for lunch and dinner, Jun-Aug Tue-Sun for lunch and dinner*. The pretty setting under the pines near the Bassin de Thau, the menu full of finesse and with succulent seafood that changes every month, and the good list of Languedoc wines are the secrets behind Chez Philippe's success. Try the seafood and garden vegetable combinations; they also serve delicious duck. Lunch menu €19.

€€ Le Caquelon, *13 chemin de l'Etang, Mèze, T04 67 74 63 81, restaurant-meze.com. Open for lunch and dinner*. This is a cheerful restaurant with a big summer terrace right on the Bassin de Thau. The menu changes three times a year and specializes in regional seafood – the oysters gratinées are delicious.

€€ Les Demoiselles Dupuy, *4 quai Maximin Licciardi, Sète, T04 67 74 03 46, lesdemoisellesdupuy.fr. Open 1200-0100*. This wonderful bistro-cum-oyster shack with a terrace is a bit out of the way by the port, but it's well worth seeking out for some of the freshest oysters and seafood in Sète. Owner Gilles Dupuy was an artist who started farming oysters in Bouzigues and his son now sends in fresh supplies daily. Save room at the end for the home-made chocolate cake.

€ Lou Pescadou, *18 rue Chassefière, Agde, T04 67 21 17 10. Open dinner only*. Probably the friendliest and most famous restaurant in Agde, and the best bargain with a five-course €17 menu *fixe* that hasn't changed in 40 years: lovely fish soup with garnishes, paté, mussels in a ratatouille, fish or meat and dessert. For wines, simply choose between red and white.

Festivals and events

Coastal Hérault *p73*

Every year since 1666, the Sétois have competed for glory in the Joutes Nautiques (nautical jousts). The sport, played up and down the ports of Languedoc, was invented in the 13th century by St Louis' knights at Aigues-Mortes; short on horses, they amused themselves by charging at each other from fishing boats. The rules are complex, but this is the way they play today: each nautical knight, armed with lance and shield, stands on an elevated platform of a long boat as teams of eight to ten rowers provide the momentum for the collision to the tune of drum and oboe. The loser tumbles into the drink; seven times the boats pass, and whoever has more dry men at the end wins. Sète alone has 17 teams, and there are others from up and down the coast. Beginning on weekends in late June, jousts take place in the Canal Royal before climaxing in a grand finale between the best teams of the year on St Louis' Day, 25 August. There are parades, music and feasts of pastis and macaronnade (pasta baked with shellfish and tomatoes).

What to do

Coastal Hérault p73
Boat trips
Sète Croisières, *Quai du Général-Durand, Sète, T04 67 46 00 46, sete-croisieres.com.* Choose between three different cruises: red for sea cruises (departs from Pont de la Savonnerie); yellow with glass bottoms for the Bassins de Thau and Bouzigues and the shellfish parks (departs from the Quai de la Résistance); and blue for visits of Sète's canals (Quai Durand).

Diving
Abyss Plongée, *21 place du Globe-Le Pharo, Le Cap d'Agde, T04 67 01 50 54 (low season T06 21 97 16 10), abyssplongee.com.* Underwater lava flows make for good diving around Cap d'Agde: learn how, go out on dives or just fill up your tanks here.

Golf
Golf du Cap D'Agde, *4 av des Alizées, Le Cap d'Agde, T04 67 26 54 40, golf.ville-agde.fr.* Flat 18-hole par 72 course and a nine-hole compact course, with water obstacles.
La Grande-Motte Golf Club, *Av du Golf, La Grande-Motte, T04 67 56 05 00, ot-lagrandemotte.fr/golf.htm.* Designed by Robert Trent Jones Sr, this 42-hole complex is the biggest in Languedoc-Roussillon and includes the international 'Flamants Roses' course.

Water sports
Aqualand, *Cap d'Agde, T04 67 26 85 94, aqualand.fr. Open mid-Jun-Aug.* Water park, offering thrills and spills. Ideal for about ages 10 and up.
Parc Aquatique Le Grand Bleu, *La plaine des jeux, La Grande-Motte, T04 67 56 28 23, ot-lagrandemotte.fr/parc-aquatique.php.* Several indoor pools, slides, saunas, etc. Outdoor water park in summer.

Wellbeing
Balnéocap, *88 chemin de Notre Dame à St Martin, Le Cap d'Agde, T04 67 21 20 59, balneocap.com.* Opened in 2009, this state-of-the-art spa features the latest treatments and a bilingual staff, all in a cool Zen setting.
Thalasso Mediterranée, *La Grande-Motte, T04 67 29 13 13, thalasso-grandemotte. com.* The biggest thalassotherapy spa in Languedoc, devoted to sun, sea and relaxation. It offers a wide selection of treatments.

Béziers and around

Founded by Caesar as the *Colonia Victrix Julia Septimanorum Baetarae*, Hérault's second city, Béziers, unlike Montpellier is still the old Languedoc. It's a mix of genteel and scruffy (although the latter is perhaps endangered by the new slew of direct flights from the UK and the house bargain-hunters who follow), and its passions are wine, rugby (the Biterrois are 12-time French national champions) and bullfights. The August feria is the biggest festival in Languedoc.

Béziers

Allées Paul Riquet

This is the heart of Béziers, a shady café-lined promenade named after the local who dug the Canal du Midi. On Fridays it's the scene of a colourful flower market. The bottom of the Allées gives onto a beautiful romantic garden, the **Plateau des Poètes**, planted in 1865 and adorned with busts of the poets (Victor Hugo being the only non-southerner). At the top, the delightful 19th-century **Théâtre Municipal** has recently been restored.

From the theatre, Rue de la République carries on to Place de la Madeleine, site of the recently restored Romanesque church of **St-Madeleine**. Nearby are the **Halles**, with a collection of arty camels inside. Camels became the symbol of Béziers after the city's first bishop, St Aphrodise, arrived on one in the first century AD.

Cathédrale St-Nazaire

① *Place des Albigeois. Sep-Jun daily 0900-1200 and 1430-1730, Jul-Aug daily 0900-1900.*
Perched on top of the city, Béziers' landmark cathedral fills the skyline, its commanding presence acting as a perpetual reminder of just who was in charge after the Albigensian Crusade. The original church was filled with refugees on 22 July 1209, set alight by the Crusaders and then 'split in half like a pomegranate'. Rebuilding began soon after, this time in the conquerors' Gothic style, with a fortress façade and a huge rose window. Inside, it's not quite as severe, especially around the ornate organ and the baptismal chapel where playful angels sit on the upper balustrade; on the left wall of the nave you can make out some faded 15th-century frescoes. The handsome cloister dates from the 14th century.

Musée des Beaux-Arts: Hôtel Fabrégat

① *Place de la Révolution, T04 67 28 38 78. Nov-Mar Tue-Sun 0900-1200 and 1400-1700, Apr-Jun, Sep-Oct Tue-Sun 0900-1200 and 1400-1800, Jul-Aug Tue-Sun 1000-1800. €2.85, €1.95 concession (ticket also valid for the Hôtel Fayet, see below).*
Near the Cathedral, this grand hôtel particulier was once the residence of Béziers' mayor. It is packed with an eclectic collection of art donated to the city, from a masterful 16th-century *Virgin and Child* by Martin Schaffner, to a portrait by Holbein the younger, to works by Corot and Delacroix. Most of the 20th-century works once belonged to Jean Moulin, a native of Béziers (1899-1943) and the most famous leader of the Resistance, who posed as an art dealer before he was captured and tortured to death by the Nazis. There are paintings by De Chirico, Soutine, Dufy and others, and drawings by Moulin himself.

Musée des Beaux-Arts: Hôtel Fayet

① *Rue du Capus, T04 67 49 04 66. Nov-Mar Tue-Sun 0900-1200 and 1400-1700, Apr-Jun, Sep-Oct Tue-Sun 0900-1200 and 1400-1800, Jul-Aug Tue-Sun 1000-1800. €2.85, €1.95 concession (ticket also valid for the Hôtel Fabrégat, see above).*
Set in a delightful 17th-century townhouse, this branch of the art museum is filled with works by local sculptor Jean Antoine Injalbert (1845-1933), who carved most of the statues in the Plateau des Poètes and the monument to Molière in Pézenas.

Musée du Biterrois

① *Caserne St-Jacques, Rampe du 96ème, T04 67 36 81 61. Nov-Mar Tue-Sun 0900-1200 and 1400-1700, Apr-Jun, Sep-Oct Tue-Sun 0900-1200 and 1400-1800, Jul-Aug Tue-Sun 1000-1800. €2.85, €1.95 concession.*

This museum, dedicated to Béziers' history, houses prehistoric, Greek and Roman finds; Romanesque capitals and other sculpted bits from the city's churches; and lovely ceramics. Other exhibits tell the history of Béziers as a wine city: how it grew in leaps and bounds thanks to the Canal du Midi, the founding of Sète and later the railroad. Until the turn of the last century, Béziers was the richest city in Languedoc, the self-proclaimed 'World Capital of Wine' – at least until the winemakers' revolt in 1907.

Eglise St Jacques
ⓘ *Rue St-Jacques.*
After leaving the Musée du Biterrois, stroll down Rue St-Jacques for a look at the **Arènes**, or Roman Amphitheatre, which is now surrounded by houses. It dates back to AD 80 and in its prime could seat 15,000 spectators.

Just above the museum, on a garden belvedere overlooking the plain of the Orb, you'll find the 12th-century Romanesque church of St Jacques, noted for its beautiful polygonal apse decorated with intricate stonework.

Nissan-lez-EnSérune

Oppidum d'Ensérune
ⓘ *Nissan-lez-Ensérune, T04 67 37 01 23, enserune.monuments-nationaux.fr. Apr and Sep Tue-Sun 1000-1230 and 1400-1800, May-Aug daily 1000-1900, Oct-Mar Tue-Sun 0930-1230 and 1400-1730 (last admission 1 hr before closing). €7.50, €4.50 young person (18-25), under 18s free.*
High on a hill, 10 km southwest of Béziers, this Celto-Iberian settlement is fascinating. It was founded in the sixth century BC, but by the first century AD and the advent of the *Pax Romana* hilltop hunkering made little sense and the site was abandoned.

There are archaeological remains here – walls, terraces, and extensive underground storage silos and amphoras (some scholars claim, in fact, that amphoras were invented here by local potters) – but also majestic views encompassing the Via Domitia, the Canal du Midi and the astonishing **Etang de Montcady**. This *étang*, a malarial swamp drained in the 13th century, startlingly resembles a giant pie chart in the landscape, sliced by drainage canals. The **museum** has a superb collection of pottery, weapons and imported goods from across the Mediterranean.

The Canal du Midi
Midi means midday but it also means the South; the sunny region of long lunches and afternoon naps, where this waterway winds languorously under a cool canopy of plane trees, past vines and villages. A World Heritage Site since 1996, its 40 km were completed in only 15 years (1666-1681) by 12,000 workers, who moved seven million tonnes of earth and built 130 bridges and 64 locks to link the Bassin de Thau to Toulouse (and the Atlantic via the Garonne river). Yet even more extraordinary is the fact that the canal only came about because of the vision, grit and resources of one man – Pierre-Paul Riquet (1609-1680).

Riquet was born into a wealthy family of Béziers, with good enough connections to land him the much sought-after post of 'tax farmer' in Languedoc. The king told the 'farmer' how much he required and anything extra the farmer could wring out of the people he could keep. Riquet was good at his job and over 40 years acquired a fortune.

As he grew older, he became fascinated with the idea of a canal linking the Mediterranean and the Atlantic, especially as Spanish and English pirates were pouncing on French shipping going through the Straits of Gibraltar. A canal could cut a month from that dangerous journey. But where would the water come from, especially on the Mediterranean side? This had been the insurmountable obstacle to the ancient Romans, who had been the first to toy with the idea. After walking in the Black Mountains north of Carcassonne, Riquet came up with a brilliant solution: to capture the water here at the Atlantic-Mediterranean watershed through an ingenious system of underground channels and storage basins.

He presented his proposal to Louis XIV in 1660, but the king would only sign off on the 'Canal Royal des Deux Mers' once Riquet promised to pay for it; in return, his family would have the right to collect tolls in perpetuity. Riquet, then in his 60s, personally oversaw the works, solving problems as they arose; after a rectangular lock caved in, for instance, he changed the design to ovoid locks. He also planted hundreds of thousands of trees to hold in the soil along the banks.

Riquet died with just a mile to go on the project, and so in debt that his family had to give all the tolls to his creditors until 1724. His canal, however, was quickly recognized as the engineering feat of the century, the 'Eighth Wonder of the World'. It brought boom times to Toulouse and to the textile industries of Languedoc, now that they could easily transport their product to the North. Traffic peaked in 1856, the year before the Sète-Bordeaux rail line was completed, heralding its commercial doom.

Boating on the Canal du Midi

Just as the last goods were transported in 1979, a new role for the Canal du Midi sprang up – that of a holiday destination. The idea that people might like to spend a slow holiday in a canal boat puttering along at 5 kph is British, and even today most of the operators who hire out barges are from the UK. The clients, however, hail from all corners of the globe. The boats come in all sizes, from a basic two-person model to luxurious barges worthy of Cleopatra, to a brand new eco-barge powered by solar panels. Firms also rent out bicycles so visitors can peddle off to nearby shops, restaurants and picnic spots. No previous experience is required, but note that once you go, you may be hooked.

The canal has some extraordinary features, although one of its best loved ones, the plane trees Riquet planted along the canal banks to prevent their erosion and cool the waterway in the summer, are slowly being cut down due to an incurable fungal disease and being replaced by resistant American plane trees.

Perhaps Riquet's biggest headache was lifting and lowering the barges 25 m from sea level to the river Orb by Béziers. He responded by constructing a marvel: a 312-m 'stairway' of nine locks, the **Ecluse de Fonsérannes**. Yet the Orb often flooded and disrupted traffic, so in 1858 the 240-m **Pont-canal de l'Orb** was built over the river and the lock system was shortened to only five locks.

After Fonsérannes, the canal flows through another of Riquet's marvels near Ensérune: the world's first canal tunnel, the 170-m **Tunnel de Malpas**. This is part of a 53-km pound – the longest lock-free stretch on any French canal – offering a very pleasant 106-km return trip, a classic idyll passing through the pretty ports of **Capestang**, **Venentec-en-Minervois**, **Le Somail** (with its grocery barge and famous bookshop) and **Homps**.

Trips on the Canal du Midi can last anywhere from a couple of hours for a day outing to a week or more. Boats generally depart on Saturday afternoons from 1600-1800. The longer trips will take you down **Canal de la Robine** (see page 42) to Narbonne (see page 41) and Port-la-Nouvelle (via Le Somail), or along the **Canal du Rhône Sète** to Beaucaire via the Bassin de Thau. It's not all daydreaming though, as there's a fair amount of work involved when going through the locks. It's recommended that two or more couples share a boat (and hence the work), to make for a more relaxing holiday. Locks all have keepers and are open September-June daily 0800-1230 and 1330-1730, July-August daily 0800-1230 and 1330-1900. Expect the occasional queue in summer but if you get peckish while you wait, many lock keepers sell local delicacies.

When you hire a boat, arrive with basic provisions (and gardening gloves to prevent rope blisters) so you don't have to race around shopping on your first day.

Low season prices for a week start at €700 for a four-berth boat. On top of the rental fee, allow around €150 per week for diesel as well as a damage waiver (around €100), €50 a week for bike rentals, and €25 for a map guide (essential for finding water points to refill tanks, stock-up on groceries, etc). For details of operators, see What to do, page 86.

Haut Languedoc and Minervois

Béziers is a good base for visiting two beautiful areas, beginning with the **Parc Régional du Haut Languedoc**. This encompasses the upper valley of the Orb, where the waters rush down in winter but in summer slow into rock pools – great places for a dip.

Your first likely stop is **Roquebrun**, a village rising picturesquely from the banks of the Orb, where a stone bridge spans a favourite swimming hole and the canoeing is safe for the whole family. Nicknamed 'Petit Nice' for its hot microclimate, Roquebrun has a Mediterranean Garden to prove it. On the second Sunday of February it holds a famous mimosa festival.

The most enchanting scenery is just to the north, above **Mons-la-Trivalle** in the extraordinary **Gorges d'Héric**, a deep dagger slash in the mountains where you can stroll under the cliffs and step off into the crystal rock pools among the boulders. From here, you can follow the Orb east to **Lamalou-les-Bains**, a belle époque spa town preserved in aspic, where Alexander Dumas Fils, Alphonse Daudet and the kings of Morocco and Spain once came to soak their aches and attend operettas in the bijou theatre.

Seven kilometres west of Mons-la-Tivalle, in a loop of the River Jaur, is **Olargues**. A lovely stone village, Olargues was first settled by the Visigoths and then rebuilt as a fortified town in the 13th century by the local barons, who also constructed its pride and joy, a magnificent triple-arched **Devil's Bridge**.

West of Béziers awaits the **Minervois**, another beautiful micro-region and one at the forefront of the Languedoc wine renaissance. Vineyards tidily stripe the pale land under rocky outcrops, and medieval villages are criss-crossed with rivers and the most verdant stretch of the Canal du Midi. Even if you aren't on a boat, visit the canal ports for a stroll, or cycle along the towpaths. If you want to swim, head north to lovely **Bize Minervois**, where there's a superb natural swimming pool in the River Cesse.

Named after the Roman goddess of wisdom, **Minerve**, the historic capital of the area, occupies a vertiginous promontory at the confluence of the Cesse and Brian. The **Musée Hurepel** ① *Rue des Martyrs, T04 68 91 12 26, Apr to mid-Jun 1030-1230 and 1400-1800, mid-Jun to mid-Oct 1000-1300 and 1400-1900, €3*, tells the story of how, in 1210, Simon de Montfort catapulted boulders over the ravine onto the Cathars, and then burned 180 *parfaits* at the stake.

To the west, in the foothills of the Montagne Noire, medieval **Caunes Minervois** is built around the golden stone **Abbaye de St-Pierre et St-Paul** ① *T04 68 78 09 44, mairiedecaunes.fr, Sep-Jun 1000-1200 and 1400-1700, Jul-Aug 1000-1900, €4.50*. Only the crypt has survived from its foundation in 780, while the rest dates from the 11th and 12th centuries. Note the marble altars: just north of Caunes they quarry red and green marble, used in the Grand Trianon at Versailles and the Paris Opéra.

The best and most unusual church, however, is the heptagonal 12th- to 13th-century Romanesque **St-Marie** in **Rieux-Minervois**. As far as we know, this is the only seven-sided church anywhere, built around seven central columns, reflecting the verse in Proverbs 1:9 on the seven pillars of Divine Wisdom. The intricate capitals are by the Master of Cabestany; the complicated vaulted roof extends to a 14-sided exterior, although its shape has been obscured by later chapels.

Béziers and around listings

For Sleeping and Eating price codes and other relevant information, see page 10.

🛏 Where to stay

Béziers and around *p79*

€€€ Château d'Agel, *1 rue de la Fontaine, Agel (10 km from Minerve), T04 68 91 21 38, chateaudagel.fr.* This medieval château, high over the Cesse, was first recorded in the year 1100, and rebuilt after it was burnt in 1210 by the troops of Simon de Montfort. Beautifully restored over the decades by the current owners, the Ecals, it sits amid a pretty park and vineyard and offers four atmospheric suites with lofty ceilings, all superbly furnished with antiques (two of the suites sleep up to four people).

€€€ Château de Lignan, *Place de l'Eglise, Lignan-sur-Orb, T04 67 37 91 47, chateaulignan.fr.* Only 10 minutes from Béziers, this ninth-century fortress was converted into a summer palace for the bishops of Béziers in the 17th century – note the episcopal crown on the basin. It's wonderfully peaceful, set in a beautiful 400-year-old park on the banks of the Orb. There are 49 airy classically decorated rooms (some sleeping four), all en suite with tubs, and a lovely pool, gourmet restaurant (open to non-guests) and a helicopter pad in case you need it.

€€€ Château de Raissac, *Rte de Lignan, Béziers, T04 67 49 17 60, raissac.com.* This 19th-century château is set in a wooded park, with a 17th-century wine cellar. It's been in owner Jean Viennet's family since 1828; he's a painter/winegrower/chef and his Norwegian wife Christine is an extraordinary *trompe l'oeil* ceramicist—the former château stables now hold an extraordinary museum of works she's collected over the decades. The large period rooms with old-fashioned bathrooms are delightful and there are delicious *table d'hôte* dinners from the garden available, as well as cooking courses.

€€-€ Hôtel des Poètes, *80 allées Paul Riquet, Béziers, T04 67 76 38 66, hoteldespoetes.net.* Overlooking the Parc des Poètes, this hotel has stylish modern rooms that sleep up to four. All are en suite and equipped with TVs and Wi-Fi. Breakfast is a delight in the sunny breakfast room, there's free parking in the garage and they'll even loan you a bike to explore the Canal du Midi, which is only a few minutes away.

Self-catering

Gîte Bastide Les Aliberts, *Minerve, T04 68 91 81 72, aliberts.com.* On a hill near Minerve, this utterly tranquil 12th- to 13th-century *bastide* surrounded by vines has been beautifully restored by owners Monique and Pascal Bourgogne, and encompasses the five gîtes (sleeping between four and eight people). There's an exceptionally pretty pool, a hammam and a jacuzzi. Prices start at €700 a week in a gîte sleeping four; weekend stays start at €300.

Restaurants

Béziers and around *p79*

€€€€ Ambassade, *22 bd de Verdun, T04 67 76 06 24, restaurant-lambassade.com. Tue-Sat for lunch and dinner.* In a 19th-century hotel opposite Béziers' train station, this *soignée* restaurant is famous for its creative Mediterranean dishes, with influences from Spain, Italy and North Africa. Set menus start at €29; come in winter to indulge in chef Patrick Olry's extraordinary *menu truffe, filled with fresh black truffles*—for an eye-watering €135.

€€€€ Octopus, *12 rue Boïeldieu, T04 67 49 90 00, restaurant-octopus.com. Tue-Sat for lunch and dinner.* Since it opened in 2005, the Octopus' young trio of owners made waves with their contemporary, original cuisine (layers of foie gras and sardines with figs and almonds, spiced lamb with a Roquefort soufflé). Two of the four dining rooms open on to a pretty patio. Menus range from €30-75; a two-course lunch with a glass of wine. is €22.

€€ En Bonne Compagnie, *6 quai des Negociants, Homps, T04 68 91 23 16, in-good-company.com. Mon for dinner, Tue-Sat for lunch and dinner.* Right on the Canal du Midi, this friendly restaurant run by Valerie and Craig serves meaty (lamb noisette stuffed with leaks on a bed of minted peas) and vegetarian (roast vegetables stacked with mozzarella in pesto coulis) dishes, rounded off with the house speciality: banana toffee vodka soufflé. Lunch menu from €13; three-course menus from €24.

€€ La Raffinerie, *14 av Joseph Lazare, T04 67 76 07 12, la-raffinerie.com. Tue-Fri for lunch and dinner, Sat for dinner.* With a terrace by the Canal du Midi, this fashionable restaurant occupies the former sulphur refinery in the old wine warehouse district. The dishes are as refined as the name, with a menu that changes seasonally – summer choices could include tuna carpaccio, tournedos of duck with stir-fried vegetables and a berry sauce, followed by a dreamy *pot au chocolat* with preserved orange. Two course formule menu from €22.50.

€€ Relais Chantovent, *Minerve, T04 68 91 14 18, relaischantovent-minerve.fr. Mon for dinner, Tue and Sun for lunch, Thu-Sat for lunch and dinner.* Choose between the arty dining room and the lovely summer terrace overlooking the Gorge de Bram, and feast on the Chantovent's delicious seasonal dishes. Menus range from €19-45 (one is based on duck, another on fresh herbs); the desserts are works of art. Reservations recommended.

€ Le P'tit Sémard, *13 bis place Pierre Semard, T04 67 80 31 04,. Tue-Sun 0900-2400.* This popular and friendly bistro opposite the Halles serves excellent *cuisine de marché* classics, such as paella, moules frites and a rich, creamy mousse au chocolat. There are

plenty of tables outside for prime people-watching, too.

Béziers and around *p79*
Books
Librairie Ancienne du Somail, *28 allée de la Glacière, Le Somail, T04 68 46 21 64, le-trouve-tout-du-livre.fr. Dec-Mar Wed-Mon 1430-1830, Apr-Jun and Sep-Nov Wed-Mon 1000-1200 and 1430-1830, Jul-Aug daily 1000-1200 and 1430-1830.* A truly remarkable, quality second-hand bookshop in a former wine cave. It relocated here from Paris in 1980 and offers a wide selection of books in English.

Food and drink
L'Oulibo, *Hameau de Cabezac, Bize Minervois, T04 68 41 88 88, odyssea.eu/oulibo/. Mon-Fri 0800-1200 and 1400-1900, Sat 0900-1200 and 1400-1900, Sun 1000-1200 and 1400-1900.* Cooperative specializing in Lucques de Bize olive oil, which is on sale here, along with other products made from the famous olives. Also stocks capers, tapenades, soaps, shower gels and other local products.

Béziers and around *p79*
Boat trips on Canal du Midi
Ad' Navis, *La Maison du Canal, 80 Grand Rue, Servian, T04 67 90 95 51, adnavis.com.* Hotel barges and rental boats (sleeping two to 12), based in Agde and Carcassonne.
Belle du Midi, *4 Impasse du Moulin, Nevian, T04 68 93 53 94, belledumidicruises.com.* Weekly rentals sleeping four to six.
Croisieres du Midi, *35 quai des Tonneliers, Homps, T04 68 91 33 00, croisieres-du-midi. com.* Two-hour cruises with commentary and boat hire for a half or full day.
Minervois Cruisers, *based in Le Somail, T+44 (0)1926 811842 (UK)minervoiscruisers.*

com. English narrow boats and wide- beam barges; sleep from two to 10.

Naviratous, *32 quai de Lorraine, Salleles, T04 68 46 37 98, naviratous2.com*. Not only do they run the first solar powered barge, the *Soleil d'Oc*, but it's also accessible for disabled passengers. Week long or weekend packages available.

Canoeing
Grandeur Nature, *Chemin de Laroque, Roquebrun, T04 67 89 52 90, canoe-france. com*. The Orb is one of the friskiest rivers in Languedoc, but accessible to all. Tours from one to three days (37 km) are available.

Cycling
Mellow Velos, *3 place de l'Eglise, Paraza, T04 68 43 38 21, mellowvelos.com*. Hire road, racing and mountain bikes on the Canal du Midi, as well as tandems, child seats, tagalongs and trailers so you can bring the whole family. They'll also deliver and meet you at the airport.

Golf
Golf de St-Thomas, *Rte de Bessan, Béziers, T04 67 39 03 09, golfsaintthomas.com*. Eighteen-hole par 72 course in the *garrigue*, with low hills, bunkers and water.

Contents

History

Prehistory and pre-Roman

Although it's not widely known, since most of the discoveries were made in the last 20 years, the Hérault and the Aude were a major stomping ground for dinosaurs 65 million years ago. Two key places are Espéraza in the Aude, where digs have revealed the fossils and eggs of some 35 species (including some of the most complete dinosaur skeletons found in France), and Mèze, near the Bassin de Thau, where large clutches of dinosaur eggs were uncovered in the 1990s.

Not only dinosaurs, but a very early edition of humanity made its mark in Languedoc-Roussillon. Traces of *Homo erectus* go back one million years, but the most important finds were discovered in a vast shelter just south of the Aude in Tautavel (450,000 BC), where palaeontologists found a huge cache of fossils, enough to reconstruct the physique of one of the first Europeans, or Tautavel Man.

Leap ahead to around 6500 BC, when the Ice Age glaciers had retreated, and the reindeer, woolly mammoths and other big game the earliest humans depended on had disappeared. New technologies made their way out of the Middle East to herald a new age – the Neolithic. Animals were domesticated and the first shepherds tramped transhumance routes still used today. They built dry stone-vaulted shelters which go by many names in the south of France: in Languedoc they're called *capitelles* and you can still spot them on the highlands of the *causses* and *garrigue*, rebuilt over thousands of years. Down in the valleys and plains, the Neolithic revolution introduced agriculture. This society of shepherds and farmers began erecting megalithic menhirs and dolmens in 3500 BC; hundreds survive today, concentrated in the Minervois and north of Montpellier, especially around Lodève and the Pic de St Loup.

Copper was mined in the Corbières by around 2500 BC, and in the ninth century BC, towards the end of the subsequent Bronze Age, the local residents ('Iberians' according to ancient writers, or Celto-Iberians) were founding walled hilltop settlements (*oppida*) not far from the coast, and trading with the Phoenicians, Etruscan and Greek merchants who sailed along these shores. The well-preserved oppidum of Ensérune was one of the most important and richest of these settlements, judging by the finds in its museum. Others, at Béziers and Carcassonne, now lie buried deep under modern cities.

The Greeks, with their founding of a new colony, Masallia (Marseille) around 600 BC, soon became the most important presence along France's Mediterranean coast. In Languedoc their main settlement was Agde at the mouth of the Hérault, which had the best natural harbour. The Greeks introduced olives, and taught the locals how to make wine from the native vines that grew so well. Languedoc-Roussillon would never be the same again.

In the fifth century new tribes, the Volques (or Volcae) and Sardones, moved in. In those early days, the Greek colonists in France were allied with a small but feisty city called Rome, united against both the Etruscans – who fought the Greeks for commercial dominance in the Western Mediterranean – and the Carthaginians – who had colonized much of Spain. As Rome slowly conquered the Etruscans, tensions mounted until 218 BC, when Hannibal decided on a showdown in Italy, marching his elephants across the south of France, having through diplomacy assured the friendship of Languedoc's tribes. The Volcae, however, were loyal to Rome and unsuccessfully challenged Hannibal at the Battle of Rhône Crossing; no one is quite sure how he managed to get his elephants across the big river.

After Rome's conquest of Spain (206 BC), old Greek-Celt tensions and rivalries reached such a point that Marseille appealed to Rome for aid. Rome was more than happy to come in 125 BC – and stay.

Romans and the Dark Ages

Initially the Romans called the entire south of France 'Provence' or simply 'province' - it was Rome's first, and offered plenty of new lands to settle and reward to the veterans of the legions. Being Romans, building a good road was their first concern. The trail had already been blazed in myth by Hercules on his way to Gibraltar (the Pillars of Hercules) and trod by Hannibal's armies and, as it was begun in 118 BC under the pro-consul Cneius Domitius Ahenobarbus, it became known as the Via Domitia, crossing Languedoc-Roussillon from the Rhône to the Pyrenees.

Today, the A9 autoroute covers much of the Via Domitia. Along the road, the Romans provided mansiones, inns that offered shelter, food and fresh horses for officials – a word that would survive in the south of France and Catalonia as a mas, or farmhouse. The Via Domitia met the Via Aquitania to Toulouse and Bordeaux at Narbo Martius (Narbonne), which at the time was a bustling port near the mouth of the then navigable Aude. This port and crossroads were so strategic that Narbonne became the capital of Provence.

After the Greeks at Marseille were defeated by Julius Caesar in 49 BC (they had made the fatal mistake of backing Pompey at the end of the Gallic Wars), the newer, Romanized towns in Languedoc (notably Narbonne) took on more importance – so much so that what is now Provence, Languedoc-Roussillon and the Dauphine were renamed Gallia Narbonensis by the time of Augustus.

The peace that followed brought Gallia Narbonensis a golden age of prosperity. Temples, aqueducts, theatres and amphitheatres went up, and life was very good for some: villas were decorated with mosaics and paintings and had heated swimming pools. Yet at the edges of the empire, Rome's wars dragged on and taxes rose; by the second century AD, people were selling themselves into serfdom to survive.

The first of many invasions of Languedoc-Roussillon by Germanic tribes happened in the 250s, but most were merely passing through on their way to the richer spoils of Spain. The Visigoths, or Western Goths, who captured Narbonne in 413, were different; they meant to stay. In 476, with the fall of Rome, they took control and made Toulouse their capital.

The Visigoths were Christian, but they subscribed to the Arianism, regarded as a heresy. Their territories west of the Rhône became known as Septimania, from the seven cities – Nabonne, Agde, Béziers, Elne, Nîmes, Maguelonne and Lodève. Their presence and Arianism made them a target for another tribe of *foederati* – the orthodox Catholic Franks of the north. In a practice run for the Albigensian Crusade, Clovis I, King of the Franks, used religion as a pretext for attacking and defeating the tolerant King Alaric II and the Visigoths in 507, taking over Toulouse and all their lands north of Septimania and Spain.

Two hundred years later (in 719), Spain and Septimania in turn were overrun, this time by the Moors in their great push out of North Africa. The Visigoths often sided with them, but in the end it was the Franks again under Pippin (father of Charlemagne) who prevailed by 759 with the reconquest of Narbonne. He granted a number of fiefs to the local Visigothic lords (who had by then converted to Catholicism) – so many, in fact, that the Franks gave Septimania a new name; Gothia. In 792, the Moors of al-Andalus attacked again, but Charlemagne and his cousin Guilhem de Gellone, the Count of Toulouse, stopped them at Carcassonne and Narbonne; Guilhem was the first to take the title of Prince of Gothia, beginning Toulouse's traditional role as the capital of Languedoc.

But Carolingian influences would be short-lived in Languedoc. The south of France was different, and it sounded different. Two main Latin dialects were spoken in what is now France at the end of the Roman Empire. They differed most conspicuously on how each pronounced *Hoc ille* (It is so), a word that became oui in the north, and oc in the south. The latter, because it was the closest Romance language to Latin, became known as 'the plain Roman tongue', or Occitan.

In the mid-10th century, the powerful counts of Toulouse and Barcelona became increasingly independent. They especially felt the lingering loyalty they owed the Carolingians was extinguished with the rise of a new Frankish dynasty in Paris called the Capets.

Middle Ages

This was a golden age for southwest France, for Aquitaine under its powerful dukes and for Languedoc and Roussillon under their equally powerful cousins, the counts of Toulouse and Barcelona. Trade was booming, rich abbeys were founded, pilgrims were on the move, fairs were established and local seigneurs built themselves remarkable castles. Languedoc had a sizeable local Jewish population, including many scholars and translators, and contacts increased with the literate, sophisticated civilization of al-Andalus just to the south, where mystical Sufi poets wrote of ideal love; others described the rather more sensuous delights of nights of wine and romance.

The elite of the South were captivated by the beauty of al-Andalus, and even as the Christians set about demolishing it in their holy war of the Reconquista, the south of France and Catalonia used it as inspiration to create the most sophisticated culture in Christian Europe, and were the first to express themselves in a vernacular tongue. Eleanor of Aquitaine's grandfather, Count William (d 1127) – who had Spanish-Moorish blood – was one of the first troubadours (a word probably derived from the Arabic for lute) and one of the bawdiest.

Ideal love was Christianized into love for the Virgin Mary, but it also trickled down into a new respect for women. Noble women held courts of love, promoting poetry, music and chivalry. One of the best known was the Viscomtesse Ermengard of Narbonne, a widow who held her own among the great lords of the land in the last half of the 12th century, and played a leading role in its culture – a dazzling hybrid that had little to do with typical feudal relationships of lords and vassals in Northern France.

New ideas were tolerated, including religious ones and, as the Catholic Church became ever wealthier and more corrupt, many people were attracted or at least sympathetic to the dualist philosophy of the Cathars. Alarmed by the popularity of the heresy (and the decline in tithes), Innocent III sent papal legate Pierre de Castelnau to Languedoc in 1208 to demand that Count Raymond VI of Toulouse persecute the Cathars. He refused, and one of his hot-headed squires assassinated Castelnau. Furious, Innocent preached the Crusade, known to history as the Albigensian, offering Crusaders not only rewards in the afterlife, but also the Cathars' lands and titles in this one. The ruthlessly efficient Simon de Montfort and the nobility of Northern France swooped down on Languedoc. Even so, the war swung back and forth until Louis VIII took over in person. By the end, an estimated one million

Cathars and Catholics were killed. Languedoc's independence was officially extinguished when the forced marriage of Raymond VI of Toulouse's daughter to Alphonse, younger brother of Louis IX, ended without issue.

Louis IX confiscated and re-fortified Carcassonne and the Cathar castles to defend them from their dispossessed lords, the *faydits*. If his barons coveted other properties owned by southerners or Jews, the Inquisition, founded in 1229, could always find a reason to have the owners evicted. Languedoc languished, especially under his successor Philip the Fair, who replenished his coffers by expelling the Jews in 1306 and decimating the Knights Templar in 1307.

Montpellier met a different fate when the count-kings of Barcelona set it up as part of the Kingdom of Mallorca in 1262, with Perpignan as capital. While the rest of Languedoc struggled, Montpellier began its rise to fame under the Catalans, thanks in large part to its famous medical school. It continued to prosper even after Barcelona sold the city to the French in 1349, after the Black Death killed off a third of Languedoc's population.

Renaissance and the Wars of Religion

Meanwhile, the Treaty of Corbeil (1258) drew the border between France's new possessions and Aragon. The Château de Puilarens (then the southernmost in France) and the other former Cather castles, or 'Five Sons of Carcassonne' became outworks to impregnable Carcassonne itself. Whenever France and Aragon disagreed (which was often) troops would pile to and fro over the border.

As the Pyrenees would be easier to defend, Paris, as part of its long campaign to 'perfect' France's borders, coveted Roussillon. The union of Aragon and Castile in 1469, however, created a newly powerful and wealthy Spain, setting the stage for long decades of tension on the frontier that only ended with .

the end of the Thirty Years' War, when the French invasion and occupation of Catalonia led to Spain's ceding of Roussillon to France with the Treaty of the Pyrenees in 1659.

Besides perfecting their borders, the kings of France were busy perfecting their good standing with the Catholic Church by clobbering the Protestants. After Arianism and the Cathars, this would be the third religious controversy to consume Languedoc in blood and fire. After the Hundred Years' War – Languedoc was spared this one, which devastated much of Aquitaine – it was ruled by a royal governor and the States General (*états généraux*), who met in Pézenas. The Catholic Church in France was closely identified with the Crown (which had the right to tax clerics, and appoint abbots and bishops), so when the new heresy arrived down the Rhône from Geneva, it was welcomed with open arms by the many in Languedoc (mostly peasants and merchants) disaffected with King and Church. In the Hérault, half of the population converted. By the 1540s it was open warfare; cathedrals, churches and abbeys, reliquaries and works of art were set alight or demolished stone by stone.

The first War of Religion ended in 1593, when the Protestant leader Henri of Navarre inherited the throne after converting to Catholicism ("Paris is worth a Mass", as he famously put it). He refused to indulge in the bigotry of the day, and in 1598 issued his Edict of Nantes, bringing an end to the wars by re-establishing the Huguenots' civil rights and setting up safe havens for them, mainly in the south.

The privileges of his far-sighted act, however, were slowly eroded under Louis XIII. The age of absolute monarchy was on its way. The governor of Languedoc, Henri II, Duc de Montmorency, led a siege against the restive Protestants in Montpellier and was appointed Marshal of France. He couldn't, however, countenance Louis XIII's minister, Cardinal Richelieu, who was systematically stripping France's provinces of their remaining rights. Montmorency joined forces with the king's brother, Gaston, Duke d'Orléans, and rebelled, only to be defeated by Richelieu and beheaded in Toulouse in 1632. Richelieu squashed any future dissent by demolishing castles and walls across Languedoc.

One of the greatest engineering feats of the century, the Canal du Midi was completed in 1680. But what should have been a tremendous boost for Languedoc soured five years later when Louis XIV revoked the Edict of Nantes. Many Huguenots had already emigrated to the more tolerant climes of London and Berlin to escape the king's brutal policy of *dragonnades* (quartering violent soldiers with Protestant families to force them to convert). Now their temples were burned; preachers were given two weeks to abjure their faith or leave France, and those who refused were tortured and killed; entire congregations were exiled to Canada. It was an economic disaster for France, as 200,000 of her brightest and most industrious citizens fled abroad or ended up in prison or the galleys.

Camisards, Revolution and wine

Languedoc's 18th century started with yet another war. Too poor or stubborn to emigrate, independent-minded Protestant shepherds and villagers took refuge in the wilds of the Cévennes. Many of their preachers were extremists or mystics who saw themselves as Old Testament 'prophets in the Desert'. They and their followers, once a new round in the Wars of Religion broke out in 1702, were known as the *Camisards* (from the Occitan camisa, (shirt) because of the white shirts they wore at night when most of the attacks against their persecutors took place. The War of the Camisards stands out as a precursor of modern guerrilla warfare: Louis XIV sent 25,000 troops to the Cévennes, and they were held at bay by some 3000 Camisards, who knew the mountains and forests and their hiding places like the backs of their hands. Atrocities mounted on both sides. The war reached its peak in 1704, and carried on until Louis' death in 1715; even afterwards, Protestants were still subject to persecution until a law in 1787 reinstated their civil rights.

Louis XIV had moved the capital of Languedoc from Pézenas to Montpellier, which erected an Arc de Triomphe in his honour. Once he was safely dead and buried, even the uneasy truce that followed was good enough to allow the Canal du Midi to reach its potential. The surviving Protestants restarted their textile industries , along with a new one in the northern Hérault – silk. Although mulberry trees and silk worms had been introduced in the Cévennes as early as the 1200s, it was only in the 18th century that the region enjoyed enough peace (and good enough transport) for it to prosper. Demand was high: silk stockings were the rage in Paris.

French Revolution actually had little direct impact on Languedoc, which after all its many calamities was relatively low on aristocrats to guillotine. The Protestants took another whack at the church façades and cloisters, and the great monasteries (such as Valmagne and Fontfroide) were abandoned.

What the Revolution did inherit from the series of Louis XIII-XVI was the urge to centralize all power in Paris and undermine any lingering regional identity once and for all. The age-old provinces and duchies of France were abolished and replaced by uniform administrative *départements*, named after rivers and mountains and each governed by a *préfet* sent down from Paris. After the Revolution, a certain Abbé Grégoire led a national campaign to further homogenize France by eliminating all 'patois' such as Occitan, Basque, Breton and Catalan: from now on, Paris declared, everyone would write and speak French.

Occitan, Europe's first literary language, had already been reduced to an oral language. Now children caught speaking it at school were punished.

Although the 19th-century Industrial Revolution in the UK would dampen Languedoc's nascent textile business, a new source of income was found to replace it: wine. Languedoc-Roussillon had produced fine wines since the fifth century BC, but the rapid industrialization of Northern Europe changed everything, as millions abandoned their farms for the slums of the great cities to work in the factories, creating a huge demand for cheap red wine or gros rouge. Best of all, there was the Canal du Midi and, by the mid-19th century, the railroad to get it to market.

The landowners of Languedoc-Roussillon responded by covering every arable patch of land with vines, only to have their livelihood completely wiped out in 1875 by tiny vine-eating lice called phylloxera, accidently introduced in wooden packages from America. The large estates were quickly able to replant with phylloxera-immune American rootstock, initiating a second wine boom in the 1880s. The new wines were so thin that they had to be fortified with strong stuff from Algeria, which along with Italy began to seriously compete with Languedoc in the cheap wine trade, especially when the laws were changed to allow the sale of cheap la piquette (eau de vie mixed with water and sugar).

The 20th century to the present

The new century found Languedoc-Roussillon and its grape monoculture in desperate straits. The cheap wines from Italy and Algeria flooded the market and led to a collapse in price and a complete economic meltdown, which left thousands of people close to starvation.

The winegrowers found their hero in Marcelin Albert, a vigneron from the Minervois, who in 1907 led the first great agricultural revolt in France, demanding an end to the sale of la piquette and other adulterated wines. Albert gathered ever-larger crowds wherever he went, reaching 600,000 during a rally in Montpellier. Prime Minister Clemenceau, in one his most ignoble moments, decided to crush the movement by force, and sent in troops who opened fire and killed five during a demonstration in Narbonne. The next day the troops, who were mostly from Languedoc, mutinied, and Albert was on the verge of calling for a general strike. Clemenceau, however, tricked him into coming to Paris and convinced him to calm the situation, loaning him a 100 franc note so he could return to Languedoc – only to announce to journalists that Albert had accepted the money as a bribe. Albert's associates in Languedoc turned on him, and his movement fell apart. Many an impoverished winemaker abandoned the land to work in the factories, and then died on the battlefields during the First World War. With no able-bodied young men to work in the fields, rural populations were decimated. There was, however, one lasting legacy of the Revolt of the Vignerons: the strength of the wine cooperatives in Languedoc-Roussillon, which today account for 70% of the region's production.

There was an influx of new blood, however, during the Spanish Civil war (1936-1939); Republican refugees poured into Languedoc-Roussillon, contributing their DNA, surnames and culture to Languedoc's mix. Many of them would join the Resistance, notably at the end of 1942 after the Americans landed in North Africa, and even more after the Americans liberated Provence, two months after D-Day in Normandy.

In 1962, Languedoc-Roussillon absorbed some 100,000 Pied Noirs from Algeria, followed by immigrants from across North Africa to fill the many positions that opened up as the French economy began to boom. In the mid-1960s, De Gaulle's government, dismayed that so many of these new and old workers were taking their holidays in Franco's new cheap mass tourism paradise of the Costa Brava, started a campaign to keep their money at home. Not keen to have them all turn up on the elite's Côte d'Azur, however, Paris decided that Languedoc-Roussillon would be the new 'Florida of France', subsidizing the creation of resorts along the long sandy beaches – after thoroughly dousing the surrounding wetlands in DDT.

Although rules regarding wine sales were tightened (adulterated wines and *la piquette* are now strictly forbidden), Languedoc-Roussillon continued to supply much of France and the world's plonk into the 1980s. Then, a few savvy *vignerons* decided that the only way to survive in the new global marketplace was to produce better wines. Applying the latest techniques to this rugged, rocky land made for wine (and little else) brought improvements that have earned the wines accolades from connoisseurs around the world. Even so, the strength of the euro, the competition, and the fact that even the French are drinking less wine (the new drink-driving laws have put paid to the old boozy lunches) has meant hard times for many; a group of Languedoc 'wine terrorists', the CRAV (*comité régional d'action viticole*) attacked various supermarkets and importers.

The population decline has not only been reversed, but in recent years Languedoc-Roussillon has taken pride in being the fastest-growing region in France; some 400,000 new residents are expected by 2015. The growth of tourism and the lure of a relatively unspoiled Mediterranean region for newcomers (both French and foreign) are two reasons, along with the promotional powers of the late controversial, sometimes politically incorrect but irrepressible dynamo Georges Frêche, the visionary mayor who changed the face of Montpellier from 1997-2004 and later served as President of the Region of Languedoc-Roussillon, a position created in 1981 when François Mitterand reversed centuries of centralization to create the modern French regions. One of his first acts in 2006 was to open up Maisons de Languedoc-Roussillon to promote the region and its products (now re-branded under the catch-all 'Sud de France') in London, Milan, New York and Shanghai: stay tuned.

Contents

Footnotes

Menu reader

General

à la carte individually priced menu items

Appellation d'Origine Contrôlée (AOC) label of regulated origin, signifying quality; usually associated with wine, though can also apply to cider and regional foods such as cheeses

biologique/bio organic

carte des vins wine list

déjeuner lunch

dîner dinner or supper

entrée starter

hors d'oeuvre appetizers

menu/formule set menu

petit déjeuner breakfast

plat du jour dish of the day

plat principal main course

une carafe d'eau a carafe of tap water

Drinks (boissons)

bière beer (usually bottled)

bouteille bottle

un café/un petit noir coffee (black espresso)

calva (lambig in western Brittany) calvados (apple brandy)

chocolat chaud hot chocolate

cidre cider

un coca Coca-Cola

un (grand) crème a (large) white coffee

dégustation tasting

un demi a measure of beer (33cl)

demi-sec medium-dry – or slightly sweet when referring to Champagne

diabolo menthe mint syrup mixed with lemonade

doux the sweetest Champagne or cider

eau gazeuse/pétillante sparkling/slightly sparkling mineral water

eau plate/minérale still/mineral water

glaçons ice cubes

jus de fruit fruit juice

ker Breton cider and cassis

kir popular apéritif made with white wine and a fruit liqueur

lait milk

une noisette espresso with a dash of milk

orange pressée freshly squeezed orange juice

panaché beer/lemonade shandy

pastis anise-flavoured apéritif

pichet jug, used to serve water, wine or cider

poiré perry (cider made with pears rather than apples)

une pression a glass of draught beer

sec dry

sirop fruit syrup or cordial mixed with still/sparkling water or soda

un thé tea, usually served nature with a slice of lemon (au citron) – if you want milk ask for un peu de lait froid, a little cold milk.

une tisane/infusion herbal tea

un verre de a glass of

un (verre de) vin rouge/blanc/rosé a (glass of) red/white/rosé wine

Fruit (fruits) & vegetables (légumes)

ail garlic

algues seaweed

ananas pineapple

artichaut artichoke

asperge asparagus

blettes Swiss chard

cassis blackcurrants

céleri-rave celeriac, usually served grated in mayonnaise

cèpes porcini mushrooms

champignons de Paris button mushrooms

châtaignes/marrons chestnuts

choux cabbage

citron lemon

citrouille/potiron pumpkin

courge marrow or squash

épinards spinach

fenouil fennel

fèves broad beans

figues figs

fraises strawberries

framboises raspberries

gratin dauphinois a popular side-dish of potato slices layered with cream, garlic and butter and baked in the oven

haricots cocos small, white beans

haricots verts green beans

lentilles vertes green lentils

mesclun a mixture of young salad leaves

mirabelles small golden plums

myrtilles blueberries/bilberries

noix walnuts

oseille sorrel, often served in a sauce with salmon

pêches peaches

petits pois peas

poireaux leeks

poires pears

pomme de terre potato, primeurs are new potatoes (or any early fruit or vegetable), and frites are chips (chips are crisps)

pommes apples

prunes plums

salicorne saltwort

soupe au pistou a spring vegetable soup with pistou

truffe truffle

Fish (poissons) & seafood (fruits de mer)

aiglefin haddock

anchoïade anchovy-based spread

anchois anchovies

anguille eel

araignée spider crab

assiette de fruits de mer plate of shellfish/seafood

bar sea bass (bar de ligne is wild sea bass)

bigorneau winkle

bulots sea snails/whelks
bourride white fish stew, thickened with aïoli
brochet pike
cabillaud cod
calamar/encornet squid
colin hake
coquillage shellfish
coquilles St-Jacques scallops
crevettes prawns/shrimps
dorade sea bream
homard lobster
huîtres oysters
lieu jaune pollack
lotte monkfish
maquereau mackerel
morue salt-cod
moules mussels
oursins sea urchins
palourdes clams
poissons de rivière river fish
poulpe octopus
poutines very tiny, young sardines
rascasse scorpion fish
rouget red mullet
Saint-Pierre John Dory
saumon salmon
soupe de poisson a smooth rockfish-based soup, served with croutons, rouille and grated gruyère cheese
soupions small squid
thon tuna
truite trout

Meat *(viande)* & poultry *(volaille)*

à point medium cooked meat (or tuna steak), usually still pink inside
agneau lamb
andouille/andouillette soft sausage made from pig's small intestines, usually grilled
bien-cuit well-cooked
blanquette de veau veal stew in white sauce with cream, vegetables and mushrooms
bleu barely cooked meat, almost raw
boeuf beef
boucherie butcher's shop or display
canard duck
charcuterie encompasses sausages, hams and cured or salted meats
chevreuil venison, roe deer
confit process to preserve meat, usually duck, goose or pork
cuisse de grenouille frog's leg
daube marinated beef, or sometimes lamb, braised slowly in red wine with vegetables
dinde turkey
escargot snail
faux-filet beef sirloin
foie-gras fattened goose or duck liver
fumé(e) smoked
gigot d'agneau leg of lamb
jambon ham; look for *jambon d'Amboise*, an especially fine ham
lapin rabbit
lièvre hare
médaillon small, round cut of meat or fish

mouton mutton
pavé thickly cut steak
pintade guinea-fowl
porc pork
pot-au-feu slow-cooked beef and vegetable stew
poulet chicken
rillettes a pâté-like preparation of pork belly cooked slowly in pork fat, then shredded; also made with duck, goose, chicken or tuna.
rillons big chunks of pork cooked in pork fat
ris de veau sweetbreads
sanglier wild boar
saucisse small sausage, dried *(sèche)* or fresh
saucisson large salami-type sausage, for slicing
veau veal

Desserts *(desserts)*

café gourmand selection of desserts with a cup of coffee included
chantilly whipped, sweetened cream
clafoutis dessert of fruit (traditionally cherries) baked in sweet batter, served hot or cold
compôte stewed fruit, often as a purée
crème anglaise thin custard; normally served cold
fromage blanc unsweetened fresh cheese, similar to quark, served on its own or with a fruit coulis – most people add a little sugar
glace ice cream (boules de glace is scoops of ice cream)
coupe glacée cold dessert with ice cream, fruit or nuts, chocolate or chantilly
le parfum flavour, when referring to ice cream or yoghurt
île flottante soft meringue floating on custard, with caramel sauce
liégeois chilled chocolate or coffee ice cream-based dessert topped with chantilly
pâtisserie pastries, cakes and tarts – also the place where they are sold
sabayon creamy dessert made with egg yolks, sugar and wine or liqueur
tarte au citron lemon tart
tarte au pomme apple tart

Other

aïoli garlic mayonnaise
assiette plate (eg *assiette de charcuterie*)
beurre butter
beurre blanc buttery white wine sauce often served with fish
bordelaise red wine sauce served with steak.
boulangerie bakery selling bread and viennoiserie
casse-croûte literally 'to break a crust' – a snack
crêpe large pancake served with various fillings; see also *galette*
croque-monsieur grilled ham and cheese sandwich
croque-madame as above but topped with a fried egg
en croûte literally 'in crust'; food cooked in a pastry parcel
escargots snails
fleur de sel speciality hand-harvested sea salt
forestière generally sautéed with mushrooms
fromage de brebis ewe's milk cheese
fromage de chèvre goat's milk cheese
galette large pancake served with various fillings; see

also *crêpe*

garniture garnish, side-dish

gaufre waffle, usually served with chocolate sauce

pan bagnat sandwich version of *salade niçoise*, dressed with lashings of olive oil and vinegar

pâte pastry or dough, not to be confused with *pâtes*, which is pasta or pâté, the meat terrine

petits farcis usually small onions, tomatoes, peppers and courgettes stuffed with a mixture of veal, Parmesan and vegetables

pistou a basil and garlic sauce, similar to Italian pesto but without pine nuts or Parmesan/pecorino

riz rice

rouille saffron, garlic and paprika mayonnaise, served with *soupe de poisson* and *bouillabaisse*

salade verte simple green salad with vinaigrette dressing

soupe/potage soup

viennoiserie baked items such as croissants and brioches

Useful phrases

I'd like to reserve a table *Je voudrais réserver une table*

What do you recommend? *Qu'est-ce que vous me conseillez?*

What's the dish of the day? *Qu'est-ce c'est le plat du jour?*

I'd like the set menu *Je vais prendre le menu/la formule*

Does it come with salad? *Est-ce que c'est servi avec de la salade?*

I'd like something to drink *Je voudrais quelque chose à boire*

I'm a vegetarian *Je suis végétarien / végétarienne*

I don't eat... *Je ne mange pas de...*

Where are the toilets? *Où sont les toilettes?*

The bill, please *L'addition, s'il vous plaît*

Index

Ey 6/12.